Steven Melin is leading thousands of composers to escape 9–5 and support their families composing music for film, TV, & video games.

Steven and his wife Natalie live in Atlanta, Georgia with their two adopted daughters and foster children.

Visit www.stevenmelin.com for more information.

DOWNLOAD THE AUDIOBOOK FREE!

Just to say thanks for buying my book, I would like to give you the Audiobook version 100% FREE!

TO DOWNLOAD, GO TO:

www.stevenmelin.com/audiobook

FAMILY-FIRST COMPOSER

Proven Path to Escape 9-5 and Support Your Family Composing Music for Film, TV, & Video Games

STEVEN MELIN

FOREWORD BY ADAM GUBMAN

To Natalie
wife, friend, companion, encourager
for always believing in me to reach for the stars

ISBN: 9781090896360
ASIN: B07PQBNQJ1

CONTENTS

PART 5: MUSIC BUSINESS GROWTH

PART 6: MUSIC BUSINESS STRATEGIES

PART 7: NEXT STEPS

ACKNOWLEDGEMENTS

Because of Jesus, I'm a Family-First Composer, #1 Amazon Best-Selling Author, and Leading Mentor for Composers. Jesus is the foundation of my life, root of my family, and reason for all success. He has rescued me from a life of darkness, devoid of purpose, and into a life of deep meaning and significance. Jesus transforms me more into his likeness every day and offers the same redeeming love for you too:

"For the wages of sin is death, but the gift of God is eternal life in Christ Jesus our Lord." –Romans 6:23

I give my utmost gratitude to the following advanced readers who were integral in launching this book:

Adam Gubman	Chris O'Keeffe
Garry Schyman	Jade Hails
Grant Kirkhope	Jack Barton
Penka Kouneva	Dane Walker
Adam Smith	Jamil Taylor
Tim Webster	Jared Farney
Matt Kenyon	Dan Hulsman
Brian Skeel	Thomas Kenyon
Christopher Siu	Richard Albert
Kyle Mesce	Chris Joye

PRAISE FOR *FAMILY-FIRST COMPOSER*

"

You don't have to grind 24/7 to be a successful screen music composer, but you do have to be intentional with your time. I'm proud that Steven Melin has fought for this balance at an early age, and he'll show you how you can too. I'm excited for how *Family-First Composer* will equip you to live the most fulfilling life possible.

— ADAM GUBMAN
(Composer of *Star Wars Galaxy's Edge*, Producer of "This Is Me" from *The Greatest Showman*, & Songwriter at Disney Parks Worldwide)

"

The only composers who make it in this industry are those that cannot live a fulfilling life without writing music. It's incredibly difficult to become a successful media composer, but Steven will lead the way if you're willing to put the work in.

— GARRY SCHYMAN
(*TORN, Bioshock*, & *Middle-earth: Shadow of Mordor*)

"

Steven Melin leads you on the path of writing music for digital media, warts and all, and lets you know exactly what it's like to make a living as a modern media composer.

— GRANT KIRKHOPE
(*Yooka-Laylee, Banjo Kazooie*, & *GoldenEye 007*)

"

The career of a media composer sits on a nexus of many skill sets: unrelenting professional development, cultivating relationships at screenings and events, online presence management…all well-illustrated in this book. Successful careers are directly tied to opportunities presented by friends, champions, advocates, mentors, fans, and circles of supporters. In *Family-First Composer*, Steven Melin helps you cultivate these long-term relationships while providing practical, actionable tips and strategies for work-life balance. I highly recommend this book to all composers. A must-have!

– PENKA KOUNEVA
(The Mummy VR game, NASA *Heroes and Legends* at the Kennedy Space Center, & *Prince of Persia: The Forgotten Sands)*

INTRODUCTION

This book is written for you, a screen music composer seeking to escape the 9–5 grind of corporate America and build a sustainable and growing music business that fully supports your family. If you read and apply the teachings found in this book, you will:

- Enjoy **freedom** from your day job
- **Immediately** earn income from your music
- **Free your time** to focus more on your family
- Experience **fulfillment** supporting your family
- Do what you **love**
- Work from **home**
- **Remove the stress** of inconsistent paychecks
- Feel **secure** in your finances
- Live **peacefully**
- Open your options for a **better lifestyle**
- Embrace **autonomy** in your life to do *what* you want, *when* you want, *where* you want, *with whom* you want, *at the price* you want, and *at the terms* you want!

For best results with this book, read it multiple times to absorb all the content with an open mind. You're encouraged to use this as a reference book when business questions arise throughout your music composition career. **Action Steps** are provided at the end of each chapter to survey your progress between each read-through.

FOREWORD
by Adam Gubman
Multi Award-Winning Film, TV, & Video Game Composer

Since the beginning of my composition career, I've worked exclusively with companies and on projects that are family-oriented. I want my kids to be part of everything I do, so I only bring positive art into our house that we can experience together. Practically, that means I score a lot of casual games and work with companies like Disney who understand that my schedule revolves around my family first. I drive my son to soccer practice and my daughters to theater and cheerleading. Weekends are set aside for my family. I don't work crazy crunch hours. A vital piece of my life is having a wonderful assistant who helps organize my business. I regularly outsource tasks because my goal is to maintain a healthy life balance. I set aside time for my family first because I only have another 10 years left with my kids before they leave my house. I'm not going to squander that.

When composers refuse to focus on their families first, they pay a terrible price in mental health, resulting in guilt and resentment. Your career should never be the focus of your life; instead, it should be the tool that allows you to fully enjoy your family. This is at the core of what it means to be human.

There are countless music business courses, school programs, and books you can consume for knowledge, but what composers are really seeking is to be part of a team; part of a family. When you treat your team and family with the same respect, it becomes a mutual exchange of information and ideas. When I develop relationships with clients, they're not on the opposite side of the table. I call them "partner clients" because we're all working towards the same goal and growing together.

Young composers often believe that they need to start their career with advanced negotiation skills, psychological tactics, and academic pedigree. Yet when I hire composers, all I'm looking for is a talented team player with work ethic to support our vision. When I sell to clients, I'm not selling music; I'm selling the experience of working with me. There are plenty of other composers that do great work. I'm selling a positive experience full of mutual respect. When a project closes, my clients don't focus on the music assets. They mention how great it was to work with Adam: "He's fun, focused, and dedicated, so we're going to hire him again!"

If you desire to have a successful career as a composer, you must be willing to sacrifice. This investment may not cost monetarily but will certainly require a significant amount of time and energy. You need to weigh the costs with your family and determine what you're willing to pay. If you can find a mutually respectful way to honor your family time, you'll be equipped to devote the extra hours to building a career.

If you desire to be a Family-First Composer, you're not alone. You're not the only one feeling lost and disconnected from your family. You're not the only one wondering how to fulfill your passions while trying to nurture the most important piece of your world. Your family wants you to be happy and successful. Don't compromise your core beliefs for a career. Honor your family first and they'll trust that your work time is devoted to benefit them. What do you dream for? Express that to your family. If you lie to yourself and pretend like these desires don't exist, you're going to breed resentment and instability. Let your family know that they're more important than your work. Then focus on balance.

You don't have to grind 24/7 to be a successful screen music composer, but you do have to be intentional with your time. I'm proud that Steven Melin has fought for this balance at an early age, and he'll show you how you can too. I'm excited for how *Family-First Composer* will equip you to live the most fulfilling life possible.

PART 1

FIND YOUR WHY

FAMILY-FIRST COMPOSER

Imagine waking up at 6AM: meditating, exercising, and enjoying breakfast with your spouse and kids – a healthy start to the day that puts a smile on your face. You walk to your music studio, coffee in hand, and excitedly begin working at 8AM – your inbox full of artistic discussions with clients and requests for new projects, alongside social media conversations brimming with engagement. Your morning flies by so fast that you must forcefully break away to grab lunch!

The day is still young, but you're in no hurry. You lay back for an hour or two: you relax to a TV show or play through a new video game. Fully re-energized, you get back to work. You pause for 10 minutes to welcome your kids home from school and give them your undivided attention; you return to work once you've had a short, but meaningful conversation. Your alarm strikes at 5PM, reminding you to wrap up work and go prepare dinner for your family – to be fully present when needed the most.

You play with your children, enjoy dinner conversations with your family, and tuck your kids to bed. With a couple hours remaining before turning off the lights, you pull out a reserve of energy stored just for your spouse and treasure the stillness and silence with your best friend. In these final moments of the day, you spend some time for reflection, planning, and reading. In bed by 10PM, an accomplished day filled with confidence, laughter, and purpose comes to an end.

While drifting off to sleep and reviewing the day, you realize that in just *16 hours*, you worked for 7, enjoyed family time for 7, invested in personal health and development for 6…a total of 20 hours of productivity, all due to prioritization and overlapping. And to boot, you earned $500–$2000+ today doing what you love! Best of all, you enjoyed your life for *all these hours*…this was a *good day*. You think to yourself – *Let's do this again tomorrow.*

Does this sound like a dream? Too good to be true? Imagine if this was your reality…

I don't have to imagine. This *is* my life. I'm a screen music composer and I enjoy every day of my life to the fullest. This is the life I longed for since high school, 14 years ago when I declared myself a *music composer* to the world. Little did I know that passion and talent alone are meaningless when building a business. Little did I know that I would struggle for *years* to make ends meet as a music composer. Perhaps my greatest fear was true – I wasn't good enough; my music wasn't good enough; music composers can't make it in this modern digital age.

I want to assure you that those thoughts are *lies*. You *can* be a professional music composer. You *will* find success. And funny enough, success comes to those who set their priorities in order. Family is always first. Then work. I don't work past 5PM and I don't work on Saturdays or Sundays. Those days are sacred and set apart for family. I refuse to live my life enslaved to work. I escaped the 9–5 grind to be financially free and to have full autonomy in my life – the power to decide *what* I want, *when* I want, *where* I want, *with whom* I want, *at the price* I want, and *at the terms* I want.

If I want to pause work and take my kids to the park, I do. If I want to take a week vacation with my family, I do. If I want to charge $20,000 for a project, I do. If I want to turn down a client that doesn't value my time or family boundaries, I do.

This freedom is available for you too. But you *will* have to fight for it. You will have to restructure your entire mindset and schedule to position yourself for success. But it's *worth it*.

FIND YOUR WHY

Without a clear Why, you will give up when the What and the How become too challenging. Focusing on your Why is at the core of any successful endeavor. Why do you want to escape the 9–5? Why do you want to work from home? Why do you want to become a full-time music composer? Is your Why more comfort? Is it to impress others? Is it to change the world?

Until foster care entered my story, my Why was missing. If you had asked me why I wanted to work full-time as a music composer, I would have answered *because I love writing music.* How did I react on the days when I *didn't* want to write music? I filled up my schedule with busy-work: aimlessly cold-contacting potential clients, scouring through online forums, and presenting myself in a very desperate manner on social media. If you had asked me why I wanted to escape the corporate 9–5 job and work from home, I would have responded *because I want to make my own schedule!* When freedom of schedule was my Why, I was at the mercy of my feelings – nothing stopped me from playing video games all day or motivated me to work at all on days when I *didn't feel like it.*

I *had* to have a day-job, where I daydreamed every hour about the *one day* I would invest my time in fulfilling work. I was discontent only earning $1,000-2,000 per month and it showed. But the moment my wife and I decided to open our home to foster children…everything changed.

My schedule, energy, and finances were no longer my own. Granted, I shared them with my wife, but at the end of the day, she's a strong woman who can take care of herself. Children, however, demand a considerable amount of time, attention, and intentionality because they *need* you.

Unlike biological children where you have a 9-month grace period to prepare your home, heart, and finances, foster children enter your home immediately after approval. Within one hour of my wife Natalie leaving her job, we received a call for our first placement – a 3-month-old baby boy. The next day, we received a 2-week-old boy. Within 2 months, we received two sisters, ages 9 and 10. Our house was *filled* with kids! Kids with trauma. Trauma requires *extra* time, energy, and intentionality. *Love* is not enough; these children require deep commitment.

My Why was settled: to love these children unconditionally; to adopt any who become eligible while in our care; to live my life committed to their welfare; to raise awareness for others to step into foster care; and to rally around those who are in the thick of it. My Why is rooted in serving others. My Why fuels me every day, especially on days that I *don't feel like it*. My Why burns within the core of my being so strongly that no obstacle will stop me from loving these children and increasing our family resources to love more.

My Why fuels me every day, especially on days that I don't feel like it.

At the time of this writing, we are on our eighth foster placement and have adopted two girls. The only limitation to our vision is our physical capacity. My next financial goal is to earn enough per month so we can build a larger home to house more children and deeply impact more lives and families. When you find your Why, no excuse can stop you from achieving your dreams.

I wholeheartedly believe that as people, we're created for family. We are naturally drawn to community and elevating one another. What better cause is there to devote your life to? When you set serving others as the top priority in your life, *your success is certain*. Once you adopt this mindset, you are no longer in charge of your destiny or the speed at which your path is paved; but you can rest assured that the path will be paved *for* you by those you serve.

In the remainder of this book, I'm going to tackle your top questions collected from thousands of music composers that I've trained, coached, and mentored over the last five years. These are real questions, fueled by real fears: anxiety, fear of the unknown, fear of failure, imposter syndrome, lack of direction, lack of marketing and branding skills, lack of support, lack of self-discipline, lack of belief, and many more.

My hope and prayer is that these questions and responses demolish your excuses – that these words are more than text on a page. I believe that these words will change your life and empower you with practical and tangible means for shifting the trajectory of your career and life…if you let them.

THE FOUR PILLARS

With 14 years of screen music industry experience, I've learned that there are four pillars that create a successful career: Music Composition, Music Production, Music Technology, and Music Business. In my time coaching thousands of composers, I've noticed that most composers tend to focus on only one or two of the four pillars, leaving a gaping hole in their craft. This is even true of Masters-level graduates from leading music composition universities. I know this because I was one of these students and have spent the years since catching up. A foundation with broken pillars cannot stand.

The purpose of this book is to focus on the Music Business pillar and to share my experiences growing my career from nothing to the success I enjoy today. See *PART 7: Next Steps* for resource recommendations for growing in the other pillars.

For years, composers have asked me the same questions again and again…so many hundreds of times that I've decided to write my first book to create a resource to point all these recurring questions to. I've experienced the value of archiving my thoughts in YouTube videos, courses, blog articles, social media conversations, and podcast episodes, so it's time to solidify them in one text resource.

Are you ready to be a Family-First Composer? Over the next five sections, I'll be addressing the top 25 questions that I regularly receive from composers seeking to build screen music careers with their family at the forefront of their minds. These questions encapsulate all the fears and confusion of building a career while keeping family as your top priority. I'm excited for the clarity and results these answers will provide for you. However, be warned – once you *know* what to do, you'll be *accountable* for using this knowledge. Transformation only happens when you *apply* what you learn. May this book equip you to build the life of your dreams.

SECTION SUMMARY

Once you've successfully chosen a compelling Why, you're ready to move forward. The following five sections are organized as a step-by-step guide to help you lay the foundation of a successful music composition career, create multiple means of recurring monthly income, equip your music studio with the most effective hardware and software, establish habits for business growth, and implement business strategies for scaling faster.

The final section *PART 7: Next Steps* will provide practical next steps to take, including building a demo reel and portfolio, interacting with community, deeper training opportunities, private coaching, sponsorships, and how to establish your authority on social media.

You're ready to move on to *PART 2: Building a Music Composition Career.*

BUILDING A
MUSIC COMPOSITION CAREER

1

IS MUSIC COMPOSITION
A VIABLE CAREER?

This question is deeply personal for composers because it represents the moment that we can become *free in our schedule*. What if I told you that you can quit your 9–5 job *today*? Does that sound too good to be true? Let's examine the same question from a different angle – what if you're fired from your job tomorrow? What will you do to ensure that your family is provided for by next month?

At the beginning of this book, I wrote that *autonomy* in your life requires a *mindset shift*. The reason you're reading this book is likely because your current mindset isn't yielding the results you desire. I've had many conversations with composers who desire and agree with every bit of the autonomous lifestyle – complete freedom and choice in their lives – but they're unwilling to take the leap. They say *maybe in 6 months* or *maybe in a year or two*…or worse – they never give a timeframe at all. Dreams are great, but *goals* are better. A true goal has a quantifiable result – a number associated with it. What are these composers waiting for? Do they truly want this lifestyle? Stop dreaming. Start doing!

Dreams are great, but goals are better.

In most cases, this hesitation is fear-based: fear of not being able to earn enough income; fear of disappointing family and friends; fear of the unknown; lack of confidence; fear of failure. *These fears are normal.*

I had every one of these fears when I quit my day job. Out of courtesy, I gave a one-month-notice to my employer and I spent every waking hour during the next month working as if my life (and the wellbeing of my family) was at stake. Can you guess what happened? Every day for a week I doubted my decision, thinking *oh no, what have I done?* and *how will I possibly match what I made at my day job?* – but then I had a light bulb moment. I realized that I didn't have to *match* what I was earning at my 9–5 job. My wife's income plus mine only needed to earn enough to pay for our collective bills!

One of the biggest myths about starting a business is that the business must earn the same amount of income as the previous job. Instead, I propose that you start a business without an income ceiling – this kind of business starts small, but your income will grow every month for the rest of your life!

CONCLUSION

Pursuing a career as a music composer is extremely viable but will only be successful if you lay a strong foundation and build with strategy – always serving your audience. Let's start the conversation with some practical steps for building this foundation…

ACTION STEPS

1	Which of the Four Pillars am I the most skilled at? The least skilled at?
2	What fears are holding me back from pursuing a career as a music composer?
3	When do I plan to be a full-time composer (be specific)?

2

BECOMING A PROFESSIONAL MUSIC COMPOSER?

Above all, the most common question I hear from composers desiring to escape the 9–5 is: *How do I become a full-time freelancer?* This is a very practical question, since the freedom of having your *own schedule* allows freedom in every other area of life. When you control your schedule, you have freedom to exercise when you want to; freedom to spend time with whom you want; freedom to work when you want to; freedom to work as much or little as you want to; freedom to be truly flexible and serve your family to the utmost. This question begs another question though – do you want to trade your 9–5 for *another* 9–5? To become *full-time* at home doesn't quite solve the problem. Instead, I encourage the goal of seeking an *autonomous* lifestyle – as defined earlier: the power to decide *what* I want, *when* I want, *where* I want, *with whom* I want, *at the price* I want, and *at the terms* I want. I personally work only 2-5 hours a day, Monday through Friday (hardly a *full-time* work week). My weekends are off-limits from work to spend time with my family and serve my community.

What is the single-most influential factor that determines your ability to have this autonomous lifestyle? *Focus.* What monthly income do you need to cover all minimum bills? Let's say you need $4,000/month. This means that you need eight $500 jobs this month or four $1,000 jobs; two $2,000 jobs or one $4,000 job. Which of these will you spend your time seeking? Any composer, living anywhere in the world, can earn $4,000 in 30 days if their family wellbeing depends on it. How badly do you want this? Are you willing to *focus* to achieve it?

I can already hear the sighs and see eyeballs rolling....I can hear the echoes of "that's impossible!" from thousands of composers who truly *want* this income but have no clue where to start. Does this sound familiar? If so, here's a gut-check question: when was the last time you sat in your studio and *only* worked on *income-generating* activities? After all, *exposure* can't pay bills.

Let's consider the last two hours in your studio – how did you invest in your business? Did you spend this precious time on social media when you could have been creating a product to sell next week? Did you search job posts and cold-message potential clients when you could have been hosting a podcast or live stream to establish yourself as an authority? Did you compose music to scratch an artistic itch or did you compose music that is sellable and viable in the marketplace? Treat your composition craft as a business; otherwise, call it a hobby. I earn music income every day – that's a *successful* day for me. I have numerous income sources, as I'll discuss in great length later in this book. My time is never disposable, so I take my time in the studio seriously. I write down every weekly task on Sunday night and get to work on Monday. By Friday at 5PM, whatever I haven't finished becomes my top priority the following Monday morning. If I'm serious about a task, I write it down and get it done...no matter how small or audacious.

No harvest can be reaped until seeds are sown, crops are watered, and time is allotted for growth.

Growing a music composition career is like farming – no harvest can be reaped until seeds are sown, crops are watered, and time is allotted for growth. Most composers expect instant or easy results. On the contrary, building a career is a long-term journey full of changing seasons, hard work, and planning. No one grows a successful business by accident. Careers are built one intentional action at a time, like constructing a sturdy wall brick-by-brick.

I recommend building your business by starting with the end in mind. Envision what your business will look like in one year, five years, 10 years, 20 years, and beyond. Write down every possible detail: How will you earn your income? Who will you be serving? Where will you live? How will you spend your free time? Deciding on these factors early will give you a clear picture of what you're aiming for – only then will you know whether you're on track or need adjustment. After all, as hockey legend Wayne Gretzky famously said, "You miss 100% of the shots you don't take".

I've been a professional screen music composer for 14 years. I still have a long journey ahead in my career, but I've also come a long way. The success I enjoy today is a direct result of the seeds I've planted and watered over the last decade. The list includes: positive business relationships; growing an audience on social media; creating training videos; investing in music degrees; blogging; hosting a podcast; improving composition, production, and technology skills by exploring new music software, gear, genres, and techniques; creating music courses; developing online communities; leading master classes and conferences; establishing passive income sources; and more. Not one of these actions happened by accident nor brought income overnight. Every action required planning, execution, and follow-through. Every action had a share of failures that taught me how to redirect my energy for improvements or learn an important lesson.

CONCLUSION

Becoming a professional music composer is hard work and won't happen overnight. However, you may already be in a healthy place to start earning music income today. If so, skip ahead to *PART 3: How to Earn More Income*. If not, you may first need to settle the value of formal education in your career...

ACTION STEPS

1	What monthly income do I need to cover all bills?
2	What differentiates me from every other composer on the market?
3	What actions can I take today to increase my composition income this month?

3

DOES EDUCATION MATTER AS A MUSIC COMPOSER?

Does college education have a direct impact on your success in the entertainment industry writing custom music? *Maybe*. This is a loaded question, but well worth tackling. Education always matters, but this decision must be weighed from a financial perspective. The best way to do this is to contrast the cost of the degree with the average income earned immediately after completing the degree. In other words, consider the return on investment (ROI) of the degree – if your education will earn you a profit in the long-term, it's a wise investment. If it will cost you money, it's a poor investment.

If your education will earn you a profit in the long-term, it's a wise investment. If it will cost you money, it's a poor investment.

For example, if you attend a four-year in-state program and pay $5,000 to earn a Music Composition degree, this is an extremely affordable option, especially if you can work a part-time job on the side and pay for the degree with cash out-of-pocket or through scholarships. When you exit this program, your expenses are minimal and you have no debts to pay. You can earn a living as a composer very cheaply. This means that you can charge considerably less than your competition and rely on fewer projects. This doesn't mean that you should devalue your work and charge less than your time is worth, but this releases a large amount of pressure. You don't have to earn much income each month to break even. In this case, school was a wise investment because it equipped you with the skillsets, knowledge, and experience to enter the marketplace with value to offer. Everything you earn above your basic needs will be profit and your business will grow rapidly.

Conversely, consider if you attend an expensive out-of-state private art school where you pay $100,000+ to earn a Music Composition degree. You may argue that this school offers a more in-depth program and connects you with industry professionals that ultimately lands you a high-paying composition job. But at what risk? Is this worth paying student loans for 5-10 years and needing to earn $2,000+ extra income per month to stay on track?

The only responsible way to compare these two paths is to weigh the end result of each. Look 5 years down the road – what did these connections lead to? Did they lead to assistantships or internships that were dead-ends or did they lead to work opportunities with high-caliber, industry professionals that exposed you to skillsets and experiences that you couldn't have otherwise?

My gauge on a sound investment is to reliably expect a tenfold return on my initial investment. If I spend $1,000 on a product or service, I expect to earn $10,000 in return. If I spend $10,000, I expect to earn $100,000 in return. Unfortunately, in most cases students significantly overpay for their education and never enjoy a positive return on their investment.

Compare this to not attending college at all – have you considered how much education material is available online today? In most cases, you can learn more from online resources and books than you can in an expensive college program. Between free YouTube videos, Udemy courses, Lynda tutorials, and everything in-between, you have no excuse to be uneducated.

Most composers struggle to grow their music business because of crippling student loan debt. This weight often forces hopeful composers to pick up a day job to make ends meet and delay progress for years.

As someone with two music degrees, I can attest that both college experiences, while vastly different, were hugely impactful on my musical and personal growth. It's difficult to place a monetary value on these experiences, including performance opportunities with orchestras, choirs, percussion ensembles, composing for and working with musicians, learning the ins-and-outs of music theory, working with filmmakers and game makers, recording with the Chicago Symphony and Los Angeles Philharmonic, assisting A-list Hollywood composers…my degree programs were incredible. I wouldn't have experienced these opportunities if I hadn't attended these formal education programs, but I also paid a big price for these experiences.

CONCLUSION

The final decision is yours to make. In all cases, you should consider the ROI and risk factor of being able to make enough money after graduation to balance all payments. Education is a personal decision that is unique to your life situation. The best decision for you is the one that keeps you from needing to earn a certain amount of income per month. A debt-free business grows quickly – full of excitement and without worry.

Once you've settled your decision, read on to create a website that solves problems for your ideal client…

ACTION STEPS

1	How much have I invested in my music composition education?
2	Have I had a positive return on investment (ROI) in my education?
3	What is one action I can take today to improve my education?

4

DO I NEED A WEBSITE AS A MUSIC COMPOSER?

The short answer is *yes*. A website is crucial for every music composer seeking to build a successful career.

The purpose of a website is to present a compelling solution to the problems of your ideal client. We do this by offering products and services that solve this problem as *quickly* and *easily as possible*. Every business in the world should have a website, not only because it's an expectation in our modern technological age, but more importantly because it acts as a funnel for your potential clients – the final connection to landing a sale. Without this tool, sales will forever be limited to word-of-mouth and personal interactions – while these are certainly important for any business, it's wise to prepare for the potential of global customers whenever possible. This is particularly true in the music industry, a truly global marketplace.

There are many composers who have built successful careers before the age of the internet and many of them still have outdated websites (or none at all), but that is no excuse to avoid building a website. Here are the top items to consider when building or editing your website:

The purpose of a website is to present a compelling solution to the problem of your ideal client.

1. SECURITY

When you visit my website (www.stevenmelin.com), the first thing you'll notice at the top left corner is a lock icon with an HTTPS web address instead of HTTP, signifying a secure URL. If your website doesn't have a current SSL security certificate, then you will be punished by Google in search results and visitors will feel less comfortable, resulting in less sales if you plan to sell products or services directly from your site (which I strongly recommend). SSL certificates can be purchased through any major web hosting provider. Some providers include free SSL certificates, such as **Squarespace** where I host my website.

2. CLEAR CALL TO ACTION

Every website needs one Call to Action. In most cases, this is a Contact button or Buy Now button – one action that you want your visitors to make once they arrive. This action should be clearly located in the top right corner of your site menu and should repeat in the header of the homepage for clarity.

I chose to use a Contact button for my website. Even though I have numerous products and services featured on my website, my best Call to Action is for visitors to email me directly. These emails routinely lead to my highest-paid projects.

3. SOLVE A PROBLEM

Most composers mistakenly tell who they are before visitors care to know more. The most significant info you can share on your website is how you will solve your visitor's problem. Make this your focal point and first section. Most visitors arrive on your website by searching for you on Google, linking through social media content, a blog article, podcast episode, etc. – they *already know who you are,* so get to the point and solve their problem. That's why they came to your website in the first place. Show them why they should hire you or purchase your product.

I have found demo reels to be the easiest solution for showing versus telling. We'll discuss how to create effective demo reels in a later chapter, but the gist is to showcase your best and most recent quality work in an extremely succinct video or audio format.

4. INTRODUCE YOURSELF WITH SOCIAL PROOF

Now that you've captured the attention of your audience by solving their problem, they've either followed through with the Call to Action or are now on the edge and need to learn more about you to ease their decision.

Introducing yourself through the lens of social proof bypasses the need to brag, list obscure accomplishments, or share your favorite food. Keep this section short, but meaningful. Two or three sentences is plenty. Anything more creeps into arrogance or worse…bores your audience. Be intentional with every word in this text – it will show underneath your web URL in Google search results. Start with an evocative picture captured by a professional photographer. This costs significantly less than you probably think and is worth every penny. A professional eye understands lighting, perspective, focus, color choice, and a host of other factors we as composers simply don't. Invest in your brand with proper pictures. As a bonus, you can use these across your social media accounts and even in videos, blogs, courses, and other branding materials.

After captivating your audience with an engaging picture, share how you've helped your audience in the past. *Avoid sharing why someone should hire you.* In my case, I share how I'm a mentor for music composers through my courses, social media, YouTube channel, etc. This is a very compelling list of real social proof – each of these items has a URL link to a page where my audience can view real numbers – numbers of followers, subscribers, and sales.

At the bottom of this About section, I share about my experience working with industry pros. Some may call this "name dropping", but I am very proud to have worked with high-profile composers – it's part of my story and experience. Why not share the impact of this experience on my ability to provide my products and services? Any time that you can show your association with industry pros, you will elevate the credibility of your brand.

The final item to include in this section is your Why. As discussed earlier, your Why is the core reason you compose music: a cause or vision greater than yourself. On my website, I use this section to share my and my wife's advocacy for foster care and adoption. Sharing your Why connects your audience to you as a person – *who you are* instead of what you can do. This is a vulnerable position and helps break down the screen barrier between you and your audience.

As a side note, don't include a biography *anywhere*. If you feel that your audience *must* know about your favorite video games and TV shows when you were seven years old…so be it. Please do yourself a favor and set it aside as a link in your menu – *not* as a feature on the main page. Biographies are a waste of space and attention. They don't solve problems and they don't add credibility to your brand. Use social media to connect with your audience on a personal level – *this* is where you can share fun trivia about your childhood and background.

5. CREDITS

As a composer, a Credits section is your resume – it reflects your experience, diversity, and prestige. No one starts with 100 credits, but every bit of experience matters and should be listed. If you're a new composer, it's a great idea to start a text document and to begin listing all projects that contain your music. You can even include uncompleted projects by writing TBD (to be determined) or cancelled projects. If you only have a few credits to share, consider writing a short one or two sentences describing your experience with each and how you have grown as a composer since.

6. TESTIMONIALS

Next you should include quotes from your top clients. Your audience will feel more comfortable following through with your Call to Action when they read about your clients' positive experiences working with you. When showcasing clients, I suggest choosing those who represent the full gambit of your previous composition experience, while encapsulating the types of work you hope for in the future. In my case, I have a deep history working in multiple media types, so I chose eight clients to represent my vast experiences writing music for trailers, television, video games, humanitarian documentaries, dramatic films, wedding videos, etc.

7. RESTATE CALL TO ACTION

You should restate your Call to Action at the bottom of your homepage. Doing so reminds your audience of why they visited in the first place and offers yet again to solve their problem. Since this is the end of their vertical scroll, signifying a dead-end, they now have to make a decision to follow through with the Call to Action or leave. This is exactly where you want your audience – the best possible way to position your brand and solution to their problem.

8. FREE LEAD MAGNET

For those who choose to follow through with your Call to Action, you have a direct opportunity to solve their problem. For those who choose not to, you need a way to continually offer the same solution. Here enters a free Lead Magnet – a free piece of valuable content that your audience will gladly exchange for their email address. When your audience joins your email list, you have full permission to send them future opportunities to solve their problem. Every time your audience receives an email from you, they are one step closer to hiring you or purchasing your product. When choosing a material to offer as a free Lead Magnet, I suggest giving a single, small, and valuable nugget. I offer my audience a free course. You may choose to offer a music track, video, free trial of a product, etc. Whatever you choose, be sure that it leaves your audience wanting more.

9. SOCIAL MEDIA ICONS

In a later section, we'll discuss the significance of establishing your brand authority through social media. For now, trust that it's important. At the very bottom of your website, I suggest including links to your most active social media platforms. As a composer, YouTube and Instagram are the two most essential platforms to have consistent activity on. Be careful not to place links to these platforms anywhere else on your website (such as the menu or linking in the About section) because doing so will detract attention from your Call to Action – where you will make sales.

CONCLUSION

Your website should clearly represent who you are and connect people to how you can add more value to them. I think every composer will benefit from having a website, but only if they include these elements. This, combined with consistent activity on social media, will keep your name at the forefront of the minds of your potential clients when they need your solution – exactly where you want to be.

Now that you have a successful website working for you, we need to de-risk your business in order to grow it...

ACTION STEPS

1	Does my website currently solve the problem(s) of my potential clients?
2	What changes can I make to my website today to more effectively solve my potential clients' problem(s)?
3	Who can I share my website with today to make more client connections?

5

REDUCING RISK AND GROWING A BUSINESS?

Composers desire assurance. They want to start a business without any risk. Unfortunately, this is impossible. At its core, running a business is *full* of risk. But there are strategies to reduce risk and to increase opportunities for business growth. Here are four strategies for reducing the risk of launching your music career:

1. SAVINGS

If at all possible, set aside 1-2 months' expenses in a savings account before launching your music business. Thankfully, startup costs are minimal for composers, but they do exist depending on your previous experience and investments. Most composers already have appropriate music gear to start making money, including a Mac or PC with a DAW, MIDI controller, audio interface, headphones, and sample libraries. I suggest stalling any studio investments until you begin earning a profit with what you already have.

2. EASE INTO BUSINESS PART-TIME

Most composers have trouble starting their music business because they feel the need to cold-turkey quit their job and go full-time into composing. The challenge with this sudden change (although very possible) is the significant risk associated with suddenly needing to meet a certain income requirement each month.

Instead, I encourage composers seeking to become full-time to *ease* into business – first on a part-time basis and eventually into full-time. This doesn't need to be a long period of time, but on average, this can be done over the course of 6 to 12 months. The purpose of this transition is to give a grace-period to fail and learn from mistakes without any financial repercussions. This time can be shortened when combining incomes with a spouse, roommate, or business partner, or spending more time each day investing in the growth of your business. Assuming you currently have a 9–5 job, I suggest setting aside one hour per weekday to invest in your part-time business. This hour could be in the early morning, during a lunch break, or late at night. Consistency is more valuable than quantity. One consistent hour for five days per week will yield much quicker growth than five hours every weekend.

3. FORM AN LLC

One element that most composers neglect when starting a business is paying taxes. Like many composers, I failed to do proper research or ask my local tax professionals. After my first year in business, I owed the IRS around $7,000, even though I had been saving and paying quarterly taxes on time all year as a self-employed freelancer. Little did I know that I should have been setting aside an additional 10% than what I had researched.

Tax laws change annually and vary in nuances from state to state in the United States, so it's imperative to speak with a local tax professional to receive up-to-date information. In my experience, I have since formed a Limited Liability Company (LLC) – a legal entity for my business to increase protection and reduce risks. In my case, I was encouraged to elect as an S Corporation to further cut down taxes by treating myself as an employee of my company. Your situation is *unique* and your local tax professionals will know how to best equip you for long-term success as a business.

4. FOCUS ON PRODUCTS OVER SERVICES

Most composers struggle to meet their income goals during their first few years of business. This is primarily because of their exclusive focus on seeking custom scoring jobs. Unfortunately, finding these gigs is somewhat random, based on your authority in the marketplace, and not fully replicable. There are certainly ways to increase the probability of attracting more frequent and higher-paying custom scoring jobs, but businesses can't strategically grow from processes that can't be replicated. *If you can't control it, you can't grow it.*

If you can't control it, you can't grow it.

Instead of a chance-based model of growth, I encourage composers to build a business that sells *both* products *and* services. Spend 80% of your time creating music products and 20% scoring for projects as they come. Custom scoring jobs will not come quickly or frequently at the start of your career, but they will come more often as you continue providing value for your clients and your reputation grows. 50% of my monthly income currently comes from music products, 30% from custom scoring jobs, and 10% from affiliate marketing. My goal is to increase my product income to 80% and affiliate marketing to 20%. I desire for custom scoring to be a bonus so I never *have to* trade my time for dollars to meet my monthly income goal unless I *want to*. This will give me the ultimate negotiating edge – it will remove the need to say YES to *any* project without penalty.

CONCLUSION

Once you've reduced the risk in your business, you're ready to start earning music income today. Skip ahead to *PART 3: How to Earn More Income*. If you haven't, you may first need to learn how to build a successful career living anywhere in the world…

ACTION STEPS

1	How risky (dependent upon my time and energy) is my business today?
2	What actions can I take today to further reduce risk?
3	What music products can I create to provide more financial freedom?

6

SUCCESS LIVING ANYWHERE IN THE WORLD?

Do you have to live in Los Angeles or New York to be a successful music composer? Absolutely not. Living in those cities can certainly expedite your opportunities to meet face-to-face with creative decision makers and land more gigs, but this is far from realistic for most composers who wish to stay rooted where they currently live. The music industry is global and we possess all the access we need to earn a successful living.

Success can be defined multiple ways. In my opinion, a *successful* composer is one who has full autonomy in his or her life – someone who earns a profit every month from music work (after all expenses are accounted for) and can achieve life goals while supporting his or her family. Success by this definition is highly achievable living anywhere in the world.

A successful composer is one who has full autonomy in his or her life.

Just ask video game composer Chris Porter, who I interviewed in the Sonic Storytellers Podcast episode 10 – he lives in Japan (born in the United States) and has enjoyed supporting his family through composing music for video games alongside his English teaching profession. Every game soundtrack that Chris has worked on has been a direct result of online interactions. From **Facebook** and **Twitter** conversations to forum posts, Chris has connected with game developers around the world. These international friendships (United States, Japan, Netherlands, etc.) have led to paid soundtrack gigs. When developers needed music for their games, Chris was the first person they thought of for the job. This is *exactly* where we all need to be.

Similarly, I landed my first commercial video game *Worm Run* by contacting the development team Golden Ruby Games after finding them on Kickstarter. I had noticed that their game didn't have music in the gameplay trailers, so I composed a demo track, pitched it to the team, and they hired me within 24 hours to score the soundtrack! That scoring opportunity became a launching pad for my career as a video game composer. To date, I have composed for 14 video games and *every* game has been a result of personal online interactions. These titles represent the global market: United States, Argentina, Honduras, Australia, South Korea, and Spain. Aside from *one*, I've yet to meet any of these game developers in person.

The film industry is more localized and may require you to live in Los Angeles or New York to break in (or have a close connection with someone who lives there). The broadcast industry is more accessible on a global level, but your music will perform best within your own country by utilizing your specific Performing Rights Organization (PRO). We'll discuss the nuances of each industry in greater detail later in this book.

ACTION STEPS

1	How many of my previous composing jobs have been with international clients?
2	How present is my personal brand in the global music marketplace?
3	What is one action I can take today to be more involved with potential clients around the world?

SECTION SUMMARY

If you've read *PART 2: Building a Music Composition Career* and followed the Action Steps, then you've successfully built a website that effectively solves the problems of your client, reduced risk in your business, and determined the value of geographical location and formal education in your career.

Your business is now equipped with a solid foundation and is ready to grow. Move on to *PART 3: How to Earn More Income.*

HOW TO EARN MORE INCOME

7

SUPPLEMENTAL INCOME STRATEGIES?

As you transition from part-time to full-time in your music career, it's important to supplement your income with other music work to speed up the process. Here are 10 ways to earn supplemental music income besides custom scoring:

1. MUSIC TEACHING

Teaching is one of the best and most flexible ways to earn supplemental music income while growing your composition business. You control your own schedule and rates. You can start and stop at any time of the year. I did this for three years before going full-time into music composition and the transition was seamless. Should you take the freelance route, there are three options:

BRICK-AND-MORTAR MUSIC STORE

PROS

1	Store staff finds you work and handles all communication, scheduling, and payments
2	Commission opportunities when students upgrade to more expensive instruments and gear
3	Free access to studio equipment and facility for recitals

CONS

1	Company gets a large cut (usually 33-40%)
2	Lessons are more challenging to stop since it affects both the store and your students
3	Limited ability to choose students (all decisions are made with lesson manager)

I recommend that you apply to become a lesson instructor at music stores including **Music and Arts, Guitar Center**, and **Sam Ash**.

PERSONAL STUDIO

PROS

1	Work from home and students travel to you
2	Use your own resources and teach at your own leisure
3	Keep 100% of profits

CONS

1	You handle all communications, scheduling, and payments
2	You must find your own students
3	Housemates, children, and pets can easily interrupt lessons

I recommend that you have a dedicated music room in your home that is setup for teaching. Always communicate with housemates about what times you will be teaching to avoid awkward interruptions. This is particularly important if you have children or pets.

ONLINE TEACHING

PROS

1	Work from home and students travel to you
2	Use your own resources and teach at your own leisure
3	Keep 100% of profits
4	Share screens and software with students
5	No need for a dedicated music room

CONS

1	You handle all communications, scheduling, and payments
2	You must find your own students
3	Housemates, children, and pets can easily interrupt lessons
4	Technology errors can cause stress and frustrated students
5	No ability for a "hands-on" teaching style

I recommend using the **GoToMeeting** app for online teaching. Teaching companies such as **Zoen** allow you to teach through their website video conferencing software and they handle all the administrative tasks for a large cut, similar to brick-and-mortar music stores.

2. PERFORMING

Most music composers play at least one instrument and this is a valuable skill that people want to pay for. Reach out to friends and family in your local network and ask about upcoming weddings, parties, and events to see what performance opportunities are available. The winter holiday season is particularly fruitful if you reach out to local schools, churches, clubhouses, and camps. I've been performing piano at Christmas parties for the last decade…none of which I've ever once sought out. Once you start playing at a few gigs, your name will spread among friends and you can stay as busy as you'd like. On average, these performing gigs pay $200-300 per hour and you can charge more depending on additional rehearsal time, sheet music preparation for additional musicians, and travel distance. As a bonus, these gigs are usually scheduled on the weekends, so you can easily earn an additional $1,000 or more from a couple performance gigs.

3. ROYALTIES

As a music composer, you likely already have music in your portfolio. Why not put this music to work for you as *passive income*? Here are three ways to earn royalties with your music:

STOCK MUSIC LIBRARIES

Music library websites such as **Audio Jungle**, **Pond5**, and **Premium Beat**, among dozens of others, are great avenues to sell your music. Whenever uploading new music, you have the option of deciding between *exclusive* or *nonexclusive* licensing with the website. Exclusive licenses earn a higher payout per track sale but limit your track to only be sold on that one marketplace. Nonexclusive licenses have a lower payout but allow your tracks to be sold on other nonexclusive marketplaces. There is no right or wrong way to choose, but focusing on exclusive licensing through one marketplace is usually the best way to grow quickly. The simplicity of maintaining one artist profile and gaining traction through repeat customers in one marketplace is significantly easier than dividing your musical assets among numerous platforms.

Try to match the style of your music with the typical clientele of the website.

When choosing a marketplace to focus on, try to match the style of your music with the typical clientele of the website. Audio Jungle attracts corporate video creators, so upbeat instrumental pop music will sell well there. Alternatively, Premium Beat is marketed for filmmakers, so epic orchestral trailer music will sell best there. For video game composers, the **Unity Asset Store** and **Unreal Marketplace** are the best websites to sell music packs.

Music libraries help tell millions of stories through film, television, video games, radio broadcasts, podcasts, and social media, so it's important to have products readily available for these creators. It's important to regularly update and maintain your libraries. For best results, upload one new track every week to attract attention and exponentially increase sales.

Music library companies usually receive a large 30-50% cut, but this is a fair exchange for exposure, sales processing, and automatic payments. With a portfolio of ten genre-appropriate tracks, you can easily earn a consistent $100+ per month. This will increase as you continue adding to your portfolio.

PERFORMING RIGHTS ORGANIZATIONS

Aside from music marketplaces, the *big* royalty payments come from your Performing Rights Organization (PRO) when your music is placed on broadcast media. In the United States, the three PROs are **Broadcast Music, Inc.** (BMI), **The American Society of Composers, Authors and Publishers** (ASCAP), and **Society of European Stage Authors and Composers** (SESAC). In my experience, television pays the highest royalties in the industry and BMI consistently pays the highest rate of the three PROs for television.

The best way to land music on television is to become a writer for a small, boutique music library whose focus is *quality music.* These smaller libraries usually consist of music editors for major TV networks, so they are the decision-makers for what music is placed on TV shows and commercials. Music placement earnings vary wildly, ranging from $0.01 to $2,000+ per usage, but $50 to $75 is the most common. These royalties are distributed 9 months after the air date of your music, so this is a long-term, back-end strategy. Pricing depends on numerous factors including country, network, time of day, number of viewers, prestige of show, etc. Landing ten seconds on NBC's *Dancing with the Stars* during a weeknight primetime episode will pay significantly higher than a full two minutes used on a foreign network at 3AM.

The advantage of television royalties is that one of your tracks can be used hundreds of times if it becomes a *hot track* within the small circle of music editors (they like to share their favorite tracks with each other). As a bonus, these boutique music libraries receive occasional inquiries from major TV networks for custom ad campaigns, usually paying between $25,000–$150,000+ per track license – offered only to their small roster of composers. These boutique music libraries are not open to the public and don't have applications for new writers.

The *only way* to become one of these writers is to know one of the music editors personally or to have a composer within one of these libraries vet for you. If you have neither of these in your network, I suggest compiling a demo reel playlist with three to five tracks in a modern epic orchestral or electronic-hybrid movie trailer style and directly emailing every boutique library you can find. Be sure to include something to the effect of: "I would love to serve your team with more music in this style. Let me know when you're available for a brief follow-up call." No one is going to bring you on their team without meeting you first. Extending a follow-up phone call will provide an opportunity to introduce yourself and share what you can bring to their team.

SOUND EXCHANGE

Sound Exchange is an organization that collects unpaid online royalties and pays them directly to the artist. Membership is free and the system automatically detects your music from published releases (through a distributor like Soundrop) and pays you monthly for every unpaid use of your music in online media. YouTube is by far the largest provider of this information as creators are uploading over 576,000 hours of new content daily! Your music is likely being used in some of these videos and you can now get paid for this. Don't leave money on the table. I earn almost as much from Sound Exchange monthly as I do from YouTube ad revenue.

Register for a free artist account at:
www.soundexchange.com

4. ALBUM SALES

Soundrop (previously Loudr) is my favorite music distributor for selling and streaming music. Its connected marketplaces (Spotify, Apple Music, Amazon Music, YouTube Music, Pandora, etc.) are the giants of the music industry and you can upload music to these marketplaces for *no upfront or annual costs* in exchange for 85% of all digital revenue (Soundrop earns a 15% cut). Additionally, cover songs only cost a one-time $9.99 per song fee to license. Compare this to **TuneCore**, **CDBaby**, or any of the other major distributors and you will see how exciting this model is versus annual subscriptions or costly upfront fees. Soundrop gets paid when *you* get paid, so they fight to maintain your catalog and are constantly expanding into other relevant marketplaces to stay current. I can also vet that their customer service is unparalleled; their team is willing to help you as much as possible (and as *quickly* as possible).

Alternatively, if you wish to retain 97% revenue from your music sales, I suggest selling your albums through **Bandcamp**. Even though Bandcamp earns a 3% commission, you can price your music however you like and there are no costs to upload music. Generally, your music will receive less exposure (and thus less sales) from Bandcamp albums versus the higher-traffic marketplaces, but Bandcamp albums are always fully editable – this is particularly useful if you want to sell an album with multiple updates throughout the development of a project, including track updates, artwork updates, or additional music. I tend to use Bandcamp as a holding cell for soundtracks in production that are of high-enough quality to sell, but not quite finished enough to release in a permanent format.

5. INSTRUMENT RECORDING

Recording an instrument for other composers, artists, and producers is another great way to earn supplemental income. These gigs pay well for your time and often book you for multiple hours and sessions if working on an EP or album. The industry average rate is $100/hr. per instrument and you can charge more once your notoriety increases or if you're recording challenging passages. If you are skilled at multiple instruments, consider recording more than one per session to earn a double rate. These jobs can best be found by reaching out to local recording studios and offering to record for musician friends online. It's important to have a demo reel of your recording work handy to share when a potential client is interested.

6. COURSES

Online courses have played a significant role in building my music business – course sales account for 20% of my monthly income. Education is the second largest industry in the United States following healthcare. With online education growing every year and university prices increasing, many students have turned to courses as a viable alternative for learning.

Udemy and **Teachable** are the leading course platforms available for educators. Each is extremely different with multiple pros and cons. Here's my comparison, having used both to successfully sell my courses:

Udemy	Teachable
Platform hosted within the Udemy website marketplace	Platform embedded within your personal website
Free to create and upload courses	$29–$399 Monthly Subscription
Courses must follow specific criteria (length of videos, number of videos, video format, video quality, etc.) and must pass review by the Udemy team	Courses have no limitations
You can set your price up to $200 per course, but Udemy will constantly offer up to 90% discounts to students	You have full control of your prices
Udemy handles all course marketing (and does this extremely well)	You handle all your course marketing
Udemy gets a 50% cut of all courses they sell and 3% of all courses you sell (affiliate links)	You earn 100% profits
Udemy pays you once a month, 30 days after previous month sales	You get paid instantly whenever a course is purchased

When I first became serious about transitioning from part-time to full-time as a music composer, I knew that course sales would be a pivotal income source for accelerating my business growth. I had already created hundreds of YouTube videos, including music composition and music business tutorials, so I knew that I had a proven audience who would benefit from a paid course. The need was present, so I began researching. I was shocked to find no courses on these topics. How could this be? A course like this would have changed my life ten years prior when I was trying to figure out how to compose for digital media in high school. I had never met another composer until private lessons with my composition professor in college – and he was an academic classical composer. He taught me a lot about music composition, but he admitted to not having any experience or knowledge working with film, TV, or video games. I had to earn a Masters degree, pay over $100,000, and move to a different state just to work with and learn from digital media composers. I knew that I was not alone in my experience. What if I packaged my decade of experience and mentorship into a course? How could this change the industry? Could this be a solution for thousands of composers starting their journey with zero access otherwise?

I only had a small following at this time – less than 100 subscribers to my email list. Realistically, even with an average 5% click-through rate of my emails, my tiny audience would have only yielded a handful of sales at best. Thankfully, I chose to use Udemy as my course platform and let their marketing do the rest. Within one year, my first course *Film, TV, and Video Game Music Composition + Production Basics* rose to the top as the Best-Selling and Top-Rated course within its category. Years later, I still yield great sales from that course (and more courses created since).

As a bonus, I've also used my Udemy courses as a lead magnet to funnel thousands of students into my other services and products – they join my private **Facebook** group *Sonic Storytellers*, listen to my podcast of the same name, subscribe to my YouTube channel, read my blog articles, enroll in private coaching, and purchase this book. Courses are an incredible source for generating passive income and for building a community around your expertise – ultimately establishing yourself as an authority.

I've also used Teachable to sell courses directly on my personal website and enjoyed the customization options and freedom to charge higher prices. When compared to my experience with Udemy though, I decided that I would rather let them handle all my marketing and management, despite the reduced prices and lack of control. Udemy has landed me thousands of sales, so I'm not complaining. I suggest you try both platforms and compare results.

7. FREELANCING WEBSITES

Freelancer, Upwork, and similar websites are practical resources for finding music work on famine days. After a quick filter search, you can easily find numerous job posts seeking quick turn-around work from skilled musicians. Typical jobs consist of custom jingles, notation, production, recording, voice overs, etc. and can be completed in one or two days. I strongly recommend avoiding any job-posting sites that require payment to apply. You should be paid *for your work*, never penalized for *seeking work*.

Most digital media composers have experience working with live musicians and orchestras. These orchestration and notation skills are extremely useful for earning additional income. There are countless musicians in your area who have great songwriting skills, but little understanding of how to notate their songs for future performances and other musicians. Help them succeed in their careers by offering to create sheet music, chord charts, lyric sheets, and tabs. You might even land some recording or production work during your conversations.

8. YOUTUBE MONETIZATION

YouTube is the second-largest search engine in the world…use this to your advantage. Whether you upload your soundtracks, perform music covers, create tutorial videos, or offer valuable insight into the music industry, these can *all* be monetized. As a YouTube channel creator with at least 1,000 subscribers, you can opt-in to **Google AdSense** and place ads before, during, and/or after your videos to earn extra income. Ads have become normal for YouTube viewers, so there's no penalty for adding them in your videos. Serious YouTube viewers can subscribe to **YouTube Premium** to avoid all ads, so there's no reason why you shouldn't opt-in to AdSense if you're eligible. After all, even YouTube Premium subscribers still earn you ad revenue for watching your monetized videos. You can't expect much revenue until you receive upwards of 100,000 views per video, but every income source counts.

9. AFFILIATE MARKETING

Amazon, BlueHost, Apple, and numerous other companies have affiliate programs that allow you to make a 5-20% commission every time you sell one of their products or services. This can easily be done by providing purchase links on your website, social media, blogs, YouTube videos, etc. For best results, I suggest passionately sharing with your audience about why you enjoy using a product or service in your daily life, *then* providing a link in a very organic manner. Always keep a clear picture of your brand identity when choosing products and services to promote – never compromise your integrity or audience trust for a quick buck.

Also keep in mind that affiliate link disclosures are mandated by the Federal Trade Commission (FTC). Whenever you use a link that results in a commission, you must disclose this information to your audience. Best practices include placing disclosures in obvious areas and using clear language to avoid confusion.

10% of my monthly income comes from affiliate marketing. The best part about this style of income is that it's a one-time investment per product. The process is simple: create a compelling promotion (video, blog article, podcast episode, etc.), link to your affiliate URL, create a short affiliate link disclosure, and leave it alone to earn income while you sleep and focus on other projects. My favorite products to sell are sample libraries – I use these every day to compose music and I know them in-and-out. I only promote sample libraries that I believe in and know will be beneficial for my audience.

10. TAX DEDUCTIONS

While you should certainly consult with a tax professional, there are several well-known tax deductions that you may be eligible for as a small business. Particularly as a music composer, you can write-off all music gear expenses, entertainment expenses used for research and educational purposes, office supplies, business events, business travel, services needed to run your business, and more. On average, I write-off $1,000 per month as business expenses from my LLC bank account, saving me over $3,000 annually in taxes.

CONCLUSION

Once you've evaluated which of these ten supplemental strategies are a good fit for your skills and lifestyle, it's time to act. Even a few extra hundred dollars per month can make a difference for your family budget, allowing you the freedom to pursue your first custom music job...

ACTION STEPS

1	What supplemental music income streams do I currently have?
2	What music products can I create to give myself more financial freedom?
3	What is one additional music income stream I can pursue today?

8

FINDING THE FIRST CUSTOM MUSIC JOB?

Landing your first custom music job is like the old paradox of getting your first job anywhere – you need proven job experience before you can be considered for a job. When seeking your first job as a music composer, it's important to understand that there are three major digital media industries with vastly different audiences. Each industry requires a unique approach:

1. BROADCAST INDUSTRY

The broadcast industry is the easiest avenue to enter for new composers and has the largest payout for time invested. It also has the most opportunities for establishing passive, residual income through royalties. Even if you don't love writing corporate music, this industry is the most commercial. Broadcast mediums include television, radio, corporate videos, advertisements, podcasts, YouTube videos, social media videos, etc. As discussed earlier in this book, stock music libraries including **Audio Jungle**, **Pond5**, and **Premium Beat** are great marketplaces to sell music. Once you upload high-quality, appropriate music to these sites, you can expect to receive payments within 30 days.

Corporate music is very formulaic: usually at a fast tempo (over 120 bpm), in 4/4 time, and very inspirational in mood. Companies license stock music to motivate their customers to buy something, so they're looking for energetic, happy, and motivational music.

Corporate tracks typically include acoustic guitar, piano, ukulele, bells, claps, or whistles. Rock and Pop tracks are the most used in the broadcast industry, but Epic Orchestral movie trailer music is also in high-demand for commercials. If you're comfortable writing in any of these styles, you will have a strong chance of landing placements. Expect to submit 10 to 15 tracks before receiving any purchases. Library music is a numbers game of discovery where those who output the most quantity get the most return. Composers who earn a living exclusively from broadcast music maintain an output of at least one or two tracks per week.

While writing for libraries isn't technically *custom* music, you can't expect to compose custom music for a TV show, podcast, corporate video, or any other broadcast medium without an *in* – an inside relationship with someone involved with the creation of a project. You've heard it before and you'll hear it again – the entertainment industry is a people business. It's unlikely for you to receive a custom score inquiry early in your career without first building your brand and establishing notoriety through experience. I'm a strong advocate of building your career one step at a time. Try composing at least one section of a library track every day and you'll quickly amass a large, quality library. Then as you begin receiving custom music inquiries, you'll already be earning passive income from your music.

2. VIDEO GAME INDUSTRY

The video game industry is unique because it's almost exclusively online. 100% of the commercial games I've worked on have been with game developers online – most of which I've never met in person. This is true for my colleagues as well. The video game industry is global. I've worked with game developers all over the world, including the United States, Honduras, South Korea, Brazil, Venezuela, Canada, and Australia. You don't have to live in Los Angeles, New York, Seattle, or any other city with a large game development scene. The internet is a powerful resource.

There are three strategies for connecting with video game developers online and landing more composing opportunities:

FORUM-BLASTING

Forum-Blasting is by far the most common approach that composers use to gain more work. The process is simple – find a popular game development forum, social media group, or hashtag and blast it with shameless self-promotional posts. The result? Massive exposure, but little-to-no engagement. Best-case scenario? A game developer sees your demo reel, website link, or free music and contacts you; then you proceed with a timid, low-budget business transaction on the terms of the developer. After the job is complete, you receive an insultingly low payment, part ways, and never speak again.

COLD-CALLING

Cold-Calling is contacting a game developer with no prior established relationship and coldly asking them outright: "Do you have a music composer for your game? No? Your game looks great and I would love to write your soundtrack!"

To most composers, this strategy *feels* like the best way to land more gigs. After all, you have the perfect solution to the developer's problem (high-quality music for their game) and they have the perfect solution for *your* problem (need for work). Therein lies the issue. Desperation is unattractive. When was the last time you went on a date with a desperate partner? How long did that date last? If you survived the awkwardness, was there any chance for a second date? *Desperation feels icky.* We can sense it from a mile away. No game developer wants to work with a desperate composer.

Does Cold-Calling work? It sure does. I've landed a handful of game projects from Cold-Calling game developers. What was the result? Low-budgets, unappreciative clients, endless revisions, annoying and unfair contracts, poor communication…overall bad experiences. How many Cold-Calls did it take to land actual paying gigs and not just lip-service? About 1 out of every 100 contacts. Some composers make a living doing this. But that's *a lot* of exhausting hours of research, emailing, and messaging…all for 99 dead-ends and 1 giant headache once obtained. There must be another way.

ADD VALUE

Imagine starting your work day to a handful of emails and social media messages from raving fans. Each message contains a compliment that makes you smile and a plea for you to work on their game. One message reads: "I love your YouTube channel! Your videos have impacted my career and I believe that your music will be a perfect fit for my game." Another reads: "I've been following you on Instagram for years and your music has inspired my team while creating our new game. How much would you charge to create the soundtrack to our game?"

What freedom! You have the position and power to say YES or NO to any of these projects – on *your* schedule and at *your* rate…on *your* terms. Why did these developers contact you? *You* are the answer to their problems. They already have a relationship with you (or the perception of one) and are ready to *buy*. Now! Best of all, your YES or NO today will still benefit them and strengthen your long-term relationship.

If you say YES, you'll do a great job serving their game, you'll be compensated appropriately, and you'll build trust and rapport for future projects. These raving fans will also share their recent experience with their friends and bring you more work. If you say

NO and connect them with another composer that can meet their needs immediately, you build their trust for a future project (and more desire for a future project when conditions are more fitting), while also providing work for a friend. This is a win-win situation every time. Long-lasting, fulfilling careers are built this way.

How can you add value to developers and transform them into raving fans that contact you? Use the tools at your disposal. Since game developers are global, use social media to your advantage. Post valuable content. Post consistently. Engage with your audience. Build an effective website. Integrate an email list. Be active in game developer groups and forums. Be an industry leader. Be someone that game developers approach. Use **YouTube, Instagram Stories,** and **Facebook Live**. Create music packs on the **Unity** and **Unreal** game engine asset stores. Create courses. Create YouTube video series. Write blog articles.

You can't do all these at once, but you can do *some*. Create value in the places that showcase your strengths. If you have a fun and engaging personality, utilize video. If you have an artistic eye, use images. If you have thoughts to share, write text. Start somewhere and consistently add value. It usually takes about 10 *touch points* for a viewer to become a fan. Fans usually require another 10 touch points before they contact you for a project. The more you can use each media type to dominate your industry, the faster your authority will rise and your touch points will increase…very much like experience points in video games.

Which of these three strategies produces the greatest result? Which strategy requires the least amount of time? Which strategy pays the most in both the short-time and long-term? Online business is vibrant and effective; it's becoming more so every year. Go therefore and *add value*.

3. FILM INDUSTRY

Of the three digital media industries, film is the most challenging to enter. This is primarily due to its exclusivity to location. Unlike the video game industry, film communities are centralized to particular cities and are very tight-knit. There is little-to-no opportunity to become involved in film projects online, aside from the occasional short film, animated film, corporate video, or social media video – most of which tend to rely on music licensing over custom music. Film communities are formed by networks. Friends work with friends, so the only way into the film industry is to be invited by a friend working directly on a project (including directors, producers, music editors, etc.). 100% of my commercial film projects have been a result of in-person relationships (and referrals from mutual friends).

Large film communities exist in Los Angeles, New York, Atlanta, and other major cities, but small cities have significantly less opportunities for composers. To enlarge your network, attend local filmmaker meet-ups and start events in public locations to gather those in your area. Attend regional or national conferences to meet those in the film industry that you otherwise have no contact with. Relationships can flourish online after an initial contact in-person, but it's almost impossible to establish a trustworthy film relationship first online.

COMPOSING FOR MULTIPLE INDUSTRIES

Most composers tend to compose exclusively for one or two of the industries, but if you're like me and are passionate about writing for all three, it's imperative to treat each as a separate entity. It's rare for one piece of music to work well in all three industries. For example, a 16Bit Super Nintendo Action-Platformer track won't work in a corporate presentation video, emotional short film, or a television promo; nor will those genres work well in a 16Bit video game. If you're struggling to find your first gig, it's likely due to mismatching a music style with an industry. If you write emotional orchestral music, pursue the film industry. If you write energetic chiptunes, pursue the video game industry. If you write pop or rock music, pursue the broadcast industry. Decide which industry is best suited for your music style and go after that first. You can always try new music genres or seek other industries later.

If you're struggling to find your first gig, it's likely due to mismatching a music style with an industry.

CONCLUSION

Once you've landed your first custom music job, you're on your way to building a successful career. The next step is to decide how to charge your clients...

ACTION STEPS

1	How did I land my previous three custom scoring jobs (if applicable)?
2	Which of the three industries is the most practical for me to pursue?
3	What is one action I can take today to pursue this industry?

9

BEST WAYS TO CHARGE CLIENTS FOR CUSTOM MUSIC?

Most composers feel uncomfortable talking about money and rates, but it's important to charge for what your time is worth.

GETTING PAST THE ICKY FEELING

In my experience, composers feel uncomfortable talking about money with clients for two main reasons. The first is a fear that putting a price tag on your art will devalue it. This is often the result of putting your work on a pedestal, a common pitfall new composers. The antidote is to compose and release *a lot* of music (every day if possible) and open yourself to constructive criticism with a trusted community (like in the Sonic Storytellers **Facebook** group). These habits remove the temptation to dwell on music you've written in the past and shifts your focus to the present.

The second reason composers feel uncomfortable talking payment is quite the opposite: a self-deprecating lack of confidence that your time or art is worth money. Sometimes, this feeling can only be alleviated by ripping off the bandage, so to speak, and having a direct conversation about payment. This will make subsequent conversations with future clients much easier. It will also help you understand that music is a crucial part of the storytelling experience and worth paying for.

Here are three strategies for getting past the barriers of rate discussions when charging for custom music:

1. CHARGE BY THE HOUR

This method is great for composers at the start of their career. Charging by the hour is the simplest way to charge for custom music, especially if you're still figuring out your workflow and how long it takes you to write music. Charging by the hour is the most popular method in the video game industry because this is largely how developers bill their time as well. Start your rates low if you take this approach. This way you can track how long certain tasks, types of music, and genres take you to compose without the risk of overcharging your client. This data will come in handy as you grow in your career and try other charging methods. There's no cut-and-dry number for how much you should charge. It depends on many variables like client budget, your skill level, the amount of requested music, and negotiation.

Imagine that a client hires you to compose a one-minute track. You estimate that it will take you three hours to create this piece, but you add an extra hour just to be safe. This totals to four hours of composing time, not including revisions. After negotiating with the client, you agree on $200 for that piece of music ($200/4 = $50 per hour). Entry-level jobs in the United States start anywhere from $8 to $15 per hour, so $50 per hour isn't bad at all. When you finish the music, send your client an invoice with the line item of *Custom Music* and your billable hours multiplied by your hourly rate. Easy!

2. CHARGE BY THE TRACK

After you charge by the hour with a few clients, you'll feel more confident in your ability to negotiate. You'll have a growing body of data on composition timeframes, a quality portfolio, and hopefully a few testimonials from the clients you've already worked with. There is nothing better than word-of-mouth referrals, especially in our current technological age.

Rather than billing by the hour, you can cut out the middleman and charge by the track. If you've been diligently logging your time, you should have a clear idea of how long composing takes you. Suppose that your data shows that the average track (including revisions) requires five hours to complete. At the above rate of $50 per hour, you can sum up the value of your delivery as $250 per track. However, you should have a clear idea of your composition speed before charging by the track. Otherwise, you risk undercharging or overcharging your client.

This method provides negotiating wiggle-room because, despite the length of the track or requested genre, you have a set rate in mind. Regardless of whether the project needs a solo piano piece that takes you an hour to produce or a full orchestral track with over 30 instruments, your rate-per-track doesn't change.

3. CHARGE BY THE PROJECT

Charging by the project is best suited for film scoring. Film projects often encompass more than just sitting down at your workstation and composing. The scoring process usually includes a spotting session, constant communication with the filmmakers, and tight deadlines.

Filmmakers typically hire composers for the final two to four weeks of Post-Production (the final phase of filmmaking before public screening). Committing to such a short deadline requires exclusive access to a composer; this crunch period cannot tolerate distractions. Filmmakers are paying for more than music cues – they're paying for *you*. In these cases, it's much simpler to ditch any hourly or track-based pricing models in favor of a lump sum.

Film projects differ from video game projects in two main areas: production time and budget. Films often have fast turnaround times and inflexible budgets. Video games often require long development cycles (usually around three to four years per game), so your work may be intermittent. It makes more sense to charge hourly or by the track when working on games. Also, video game budgets are far less certain, especially in the indie world and anywhere crowdfunding is involved.

When you say YES to something, you're always saying NO to more.

Of course, this begs the question: "How much should I charge for this project?" I was recently booked for three weeks to score a documentary. I asked myself: "What is the baseline income I need to earn during these three weeks?" Remember, when you say YES to something, you're saying NO to more. Make your commitments count. Be proud to represent your work.

My next question was: "What are my major needs this month that will move the needle forward in my business?" My answer was to upgrade music gear and build a custom PC to replace my trusty iMac that had recently bit the dust. It was also my wife's birthday during that month, and I wanted to set aside funds to spend on her. With these expenses in mind, I was armed with my Why when entering the project negotiation. It turned out that my price was higher than what the film team had budgeted, but because I presented my case, they agreed and paid the amount I requested. This tactic works!

SEPARATE FEES AS LINE ITEMS

Whenever possible, separate your creative fee from a music gear or production fee. In this recent documentary project, I not only charged for my time (the final music delivery), but also for sample instruments that were required to make the project great. My invoice reflected this with two separate fees: *music production* and *composition*. The latter covered my time and work, while the former covered the actual gear I needed to create the best product possible.

NEGOTIATING HIGH GROUND

Business transactions are never neutral; there is always a dominant party. When a client needs you more than you need their money, you are in the driver's seat. Oftentimes, this is revealed by who speaks first. When you approach a client, you are subject to their wishes, price points, and desires. When they approach *you,* you have the negotiating high ground.

If you name a price that's grossly under the budget of the developer, they will leap with glee at that deal knowing they're paying less than they had planned (and probably less than your time is worth). When they mention their budget first, you're in a much better position to know their expectations and how to respond with a strategy to both help them and get compensated fairly. Even if your rate is considerably higher than their expectation, this positions you as the expert. It's not always possible for beginning composers to be in this position, but it is certainly the most powerful way to get paid for what your time is worth.

CONCLUSION

Once you decide how to charge your clients, you'll have the means and confidence to grow your business. If you want to grow even faster, increase your custom music rates…

ACTION STEPS

1	Which method have I used to charge clients for my past three projects (if applicable)?
2	What is one hour of my time worth in the marketplace today (choose a specific dollar amount)?
3	What is one step I can take today to position my brand more effectively so that potential clients will approach me for more gigs?

10

INCREASING CUSTOM MUSIC RATES?

Every composer wants to know how to increase custom music rates and grow their business. I don't believe that *value* is the issue here, but rather backlash from clients. Perhaps you once had the confidence to ask for a high rate on a project, but you were shot down by a prospective client. This may have occurred multiple times, causing insecurities to flood in. Fears of all kinds – from feeling inadequate to doubting that your music is worth charging a high rate – have trapped you into a rate that is hurting your business, not growing it. You now lack the confidence to charge what your time is worth. Thankfully, the solution is quick and simple…but not easy!

How do you increase your rates? Just do it. I suggest that you increase your rates by 30% *today*. Yep, you read that correctly – *thirty* percent! Studies show that your clients won't even notice the difference. And to the few that do notice, they are likely in your bottom 20% of clientele that aren't worth pursuing further. Those are the clients who communicate poorly, expect high results for low payment, and demand the bulk of your time.

For example, a new composer who has only written for a few projects and normally charges $500 per minute of custom music can increase by 30% to $650 per minute. His clients won't feel the weight of the change, but the composer's wallet will feel a significant change after working on a few projects.

Why are we able to increase by this amount? We must understand the *value proposition* of our music. Based on current surveys of composers in the United States in 2019, the industry average rate for custom music is between \$500 – \$1,500 per minute of finished audio. It makes sense that a composer who lacks the experience, skillset, speed, and tools will charge in the lower tier of that range.

If you've been composing for a while and aren't comfortable with the low rate you're charging, bump it up! Charge 30% more on your next project. Stretch your comfort zone. You'll be shocked by how little resistance you'll receive. In fact, I encourage you to increase your rate by 30% *every project* until you hit resistance; at that point, you can scale back to meet your client's budget if your schedule allows for it. You'll never know how much your music is worth in the marketplace until you dare to challenge your expectations.

In the case of repeat clients, I do suggest politely explaining before a rate increase. You never want to damage relationships in the process of business growth. If you have already committed to a large project at a previous rate, finish it and increase for the next. Your integrity is everything in business; don't trade it for a quick buck.

You'll never know how much your music is worth in the marketplace until you dare to challenge your expectations.

I was recently approached by a game developer to score his game trailer. He needed two minutes of music, so I quoted \$2,000 for the small project. A few years ago, I would have been petrified to ask for that much. I was afraid of rejection and didn't want to receive a NO. After over a decade of projects, I've learned to quote the amount that I know my time is worth (usually with a 30% increase added on top for negotiating room).

I compose at an industry-standard speed of one-minute of finished music per three hours of work. I finished this project in two days, investing a total of six hours for $2,000 – an hourly rate of $333. Not bad! I'm currently working towards a rate of $1,000 per hour so I can focus on less projects per week and give more attention to each.

CONCLUSION

Now that you've learned how to increase your rates, it's time to do it. There's also one more viable recurring income stream to discuss…

ACTION STEPS

1	When was the last time I increased my custom music rate?
2	When was the last time I received resistance from my proposed custom music rate?
3	What is stopping me from increasing my rate 30% on my next project?

11

EARNING REAL INCOME FROM MUSIC STREAMING?

Over the last three years, I've had over 800,000 streams on Spotify alone. This amounts to about $5,000 income, which breaks down to a steady $130 or so per month with only an 8% margin of change from month to month (that's extremely steady). Only 10% of these streams is from original music, but 90% is from covers of video game music. This isn't a ton of money and certainly isn't enough to live from, but music streaming is one of the many sources of passive income we can setup for recurring, predictable earnings each month.

Uploading music to streaming services has never been easier and only takes about 20 minutes to upload an entire album. As discussed earlier, **Soundrop** is my favorite streaming distributor because it costs nothing to upload music and they only take a 15% cut on the back-end. Most other distributors cost up-front fees and are poor business models for starting composers. Even with my established music library, I earn more income through Soundrop than I have with **TuneCore** or **CDBaby**.

There has been an incredible amount of negativity from artists over the last decade complaining about how streaming services have devalued music and how we should avoid feeding the model…but this way of thinking is contrary to how technology grows. Every new technological innovation has negated previous technologies (such as how the radio replaced the newspaper, the television replaced the radio, and Netflix and Hulu have since replaced television). The day of CD's and renting Blockbuster videos has passed. Physical media is a dying breed and is almost extinct, aside from collection products. As a consumer, I prefer digital streaming and I can't tell you the last soundtrack I bought.

It's no surprise that the ease and wide accessibility of streamed music has crushed physical music sales. Instead of standing still and wishing for the ways of the past to return, we might as well benefit from what is here now – even if it's a fraction of previous earnings.

With over 30 streaming platforms on the market, **Spotify** gives the best compensation to artists in the long-run. Spotify pays artists $0.00397 (40% of one penny) per stream. Of course this sounds incredibly low, but this is a fair rate considering the thousands of streams you can expect per month. **Apple Music** pays $0.00783, about double that of Spotify and 6 times that of **Pandora** at $0.00134, yet there is a considerable difference in the market share percentage among platforms.

> **We might as well benefit from what is here now – even if it's a fraction of previous earnings.**

It's important to note that Spotify owns 47% of the market, while its top competitors only own 21% (Pandora) and 11% (Apple Music). The remaining platforms duke out the leftover 21%. This factor alone is enough evidence to ignore all other stores, including **Google Play, Amazon Music, Deezer**, and **Rhapsody**. Even though a service like **Akazoo** will pay $0.53026 (53 cents!) per stream, it owns less than 0.01% of the music streaming market.

YouTube is the oddball the bunch because it has traditionally been a video streaming platform. YouTube ad revenue rates have always been extremely low, at $0.00074 (7% of one penny) per video view. **YouTube Music** has recently launched and is proving to be a sizeable force in the music streaming space. Time will tell how effective it is, but YouTube does own 8% of the streaming market and will surely rise given its strong integration into streaming distributors.

The average monthly minimum wage in the United States is currently $1,472. If we average how many streams it will take to reach this income, this is a fair way to judge which platform will be the best investment for you:

Spotify	370,000 streams
Apple Music	187,000 streams
Pandora	1,098,500 streams
YouTube	1,989,000 streams

That's right – it will take 1.9 million streams on YouTube to reach minimum wage! Spotify currently has 159 million active users and 71 million are paid subscribers. Spotify projects to have 100 million paying subscribers by 2020. There are 30 million songs on Spotify and 20,000 new songs are added daily. 52% of Spotify listeners are listening on their phone.

As a composer, you want your music to be heard. In a traditional sales model, you may choose to upload your music to a personal website, **Soundcloud**, **Bandcamp**, or another source where you're not being paid for each listen. In those scenarios, your greatest hope is for someone to purchase a song or an album. Without an active and established fanbase, you'll have a hard time earning sales. Compare this to streaming where your audience can consume your music for free. As technology continues improving, music streaming frequency and quantity is bound to increase.

Consider cars that are now equipped with Wi-Fi. In just five years, we'll be even more connected to the Internet without the excuse of poor data or long loading times. Self-driving cars will free up more time and attention for music and video streaming. We live in a world that is constantly changing and your music needs to be in the best possible place to be heard.

Thankfully, when you upload your music to a streaming distributor like Soundrop, you are given the option to distribute your music to multiple streaming platforms at no additional cost. In one click, you can upload your album to all the major platforms including Spotify, Apple Music, Pandora, YouTube Music, Amazon Music, Deezer, etc…for *free!* In my experience, I believe that Spotify will give you the best rate of return, but I don't have to choose. When I upload my music, I reap the benefits of each service and have the freedom to deselect any of the streaming platforms I don't want to support – this could be advantageous if you want your fan base to stream exclusively from select platforms.

When building your streaming audience from scratch, I suggest starting with cover music. Yes, you will have to pay a small license fee on the front-end for each track, but having a database of highly-searched songs will help build your followers quickly. Then when you release an original album, you'll have a following that listens. Most composers only release original music and wonder why they never get many streams. Just like when building an audience on YouTube or social media, it's important to draw people in with something they connect with, *then* offer your original material.

ACTION STEPS

1	How much of my music portfolio is actively streaming?
2	How much of my streaming music is original? How much is cover music?
3	What is one action I can take today to upload more of my music for streaming?

SECTION SUMMARY

If you've read *PART 3: How to Earn More Income* and followed the Action Steps, then you've successfully added supplemental music income to your business, landed your first custom music job, determined the best method for charging your clients, increased your custom music rates, and are actively earning income from music streaming.

Now that your composition business is earning income, you're ready to increase the quality of your music with more effective studio gear. Move on to *PART 4: Best Tools for Composing*.

BEST TOOLS FOR COMPOSING

12

BEST DAW FOR COMPOSING MUSIC?

I'm still surprised by how often I receive this question from composers – as if one Digital Audio Workstation (DAW) rules them all and is built for all purposes. Unfortunately, this is far from true. Each DAW has a unique purpose, intention, and functionality. There is a great amount of overlap across DAWs (they all basically do the same thing), but the nuances of each are useful when writing for particular media and styles.

Every DAW can record audio, notate Musical Instrument Digital Interface (MIDI), organize music data, and export in multiple audio formats. Every DAW includes default plugins for mixing, such as reverb, compressors, and equalizers (EQ). Some DAWs include default sample instruments, notation software integration, and film scoring capabilities. Each DAW does this differently and caters to a specific type of composition. Here are the top DAWs in the industry and why you should consider adding them to your arsenal. For simplicity of comparison, I've limited each DAW to 3 pros and cons:

LOGIC PRO

Logic Pro by Apple is the one Mac-only DAW on this list. It has the appearance of *Garage Band Pro*, but don't let that fool you. Logic is easy to access, but difficult to master. Its menus have sub-menus and those sub-menus have menus. Upon first open, I suggest ticking the *Advanced* checkbox within the Preferences menu to view the expanded version of the DAW, revealing numerous useful hidden functions. Logic is by far the most budget-friendly DAW for Mac users due to its inclusion of a massive sample instrument and plugin library (most notably the *EXS24* sampler, Drummer, synth engines, orchestral instruments, rock instruments, and ethnic instruments).

PROS

1	Logic has fully-customizable key commands.
2	Logic has a unique Capture Recording function that can capture any recent performance if you forget to hit the record button. This has saved me countless times when improvising on a keyboard.
3	MIDI editing and Automation functions are organized.

CONS

1	Logic is only available for Mac.
2	Advanced functions are difficult to find.
3	Editing audio is frustrating and batch track actions are limited.

DIGITAL PERFORMER

Digital Performer by MOTU is another industry-leading DAW, packed with extremely deep features for improving your workflow speed. DP has a very steep learning curve but is well worth the time investment. DP has more search functionality than any other DAW and is highly equipped for film scoring, with advanced features for scoring infinite scenes (or tracks) per session through V-Racks and Chunks menus. If you plan on composing multiple tracks for a project (movie, album, episodes, etc.), DP's unique resource sharing will save you countless hours working on multiple tracks within one session.

PROS

1	Full customization: From key commands, color options, document setup, editing preferences, layouts, automation, etc. – Digital Performer is fully customizable from head to toe.
2	Search is where DP shines most. Want to record an Oboe trill? Type "Ob…" in the instrument search bar and all the Oboe patches in your template will appear, ready to be recorded. Want to sort your film scenes by those that are emotional? Type "emot…" in the Chunks search bar and it will filter all your cue track Chunks down to those you labeled with "emotional". Search is an incredible tool for composing quickly in a DAW. I use DP search bars constantly.
3	DP is the most advanced DAW for film scoring due to its unique ability to divide videos into infinite scenes, all within one session. Each scene can share as many tracks, sample instruments, plugins, and channels as desired through the use of V-Racks and Chunks menus.

CONS

1	DP is the most expensive DAW on the market if it's your *first* DAW purchase. However, a cross-grade license is available for a significant discount when you provide MOTU with a valid serial number from another DAW when purchasing.
2	Digital Performer uses its own terminology for every audio, MIDI, plugin, and editing item – this is extremely confusing if DP is *not* your first DAW. The default key commands and document setup options are impractical for the ideal user (film composer) and will need a complete overhaul upon first open.
3	All DP's editing functions are divided by tools and tabs, so there is a great amount of switching between these when editing. A fast workflow can certainly be obtained once these procedures are learned but may be frustrating for a few weeks while learning.

PRO TOOLS

Pro Tools by Avid is universally heralded as the industry standard DAW for audio editing and mixing. Pro Tools can be found in almost every recording studio across the globe because of its unparalleled audio editing functions. With one command, you can export all regions as separate audio files; with one stroke of the mouse, you can batch trim or extend all selected tracks; when bouncing offline, Pro Tools can export audio at over 100 times playback speed. Not only this – Pro Tools also has film scoring, deep mixing functions, and real-time Audio Suite plugins. Pro Tools is a must-have DAW for any composer who plans to work with live audio.

PROS

1	Pro Tools is the best DAW on the market for editing audio quickly, cleanly, and efficiently. Its batch editing functions are unparalleled.
2	PT's clean interface and quick-loading functions promote a fast workflow.
3	PT is used around the world in almost every music studio. This makes file-sharing and collaborating effortless.

CONS

1	Pro Tools is terrible at MIDI recording and editing. From clunky inputs and confusing routings to hidden, overly complex functions, Pro Tools is arguably the worst DAW for composing with MIDI.
2	PT is one of the most expensive DAWs. I don't recommend it for composers who work mostly with MIDI.
3	PT has a poor selection of default sample instruments and plugins. Third-party plugins will be needed.

CUBASE

Cubase by Steinberg is a beloved DAW by composers of all fields, due to its unique blend of Logic Pro's easy MIDI editing, Digital Performer's deep organization features, and Pro Tools' clean audio editing. When comparing all these DAWs, feature placement and workflow will ultimately determine your preference. Cubase is my go-to DAW for fast composing in an empty session due to its ability to load new instruments quickly and in bulk.

PROS

1	MIDI and audio tracks are easy to edit.
2	Organization features are expansive and unique.
3	Cubase has great default sample instruments and plugins.

CONS

1	Film scoring features are limited.
2	Mixing options are limited.
3	Window and track customization is limited.

LIVE

Live by Ableton is a one-of-a-kind DAW, focusing on vertical sequencing rather than traditional horizontal sequencing. Originally created for DJ's, Live revolves around triggering regions, often used as samples or loops in a live setting. Once a region has been created in one of the vertical instrument rows, it can be triggered at any time alongside other regions. When the Record button is enabled, an entire performance can be sequenced from the vertical editor into the corresponding horizontal editor. This is a powerful and inspiring way to compose long tracks in one sitting, including dance music, ambient music, and improvised tracks. Both vertical or horizontal region selections can be exported as audio tracks for optimum flexibility. Ableton Live remains my favorite DAW to compose loops or layers in.

The closest competitor to Live is **FL Studio,** which focuses on a similar composition approach, but with drum beat creation as a focal point. I recommend Live over FL Studio since all its looping and interface functions are more useful for screen music composition.

PROS

1	Live has unique vertical sequencing for DJ-like region triggering.
2	Live is the fastest DAW for composing quick MIDI tracks.
3	The horizontal sequencing window can be used to quickly convert a vertical-sequenced loop into a horizontal track.

CONS

1	Live has extremely limited audio editing, but has unique audio looping, audio-to-MIDI conversion, tempo stretching, and more.
2	Live excels at vertical sequencing but suffers at horizontal sequencing as a result. Live is not designed to function like a standard DAW, so many of the standard MIDI and audio input and editing functions are missing.
3	While Live can load a video to score, it has very limited options due to its division of vertical and horizontal sequencing (film is by nature a horizontal medium). I recommend any other video-capable DAW for film scoring.

REAPER

Reaper is the most cost-effective DAW on the market. It has all the basic functionality of the previously mentioned DAWs, but without the price tag. Reaper has two price points: a $60 discounted license for personal use (or if you earn less than $20,000 per year with it commercially), and a $225 commercial license. Reaper also offers a 60-day trial period, which is plenty of time to learn the environment and decide if it's the right DAW for you.

Reaper is best-known for its full customization control and unique scripting language (ReaScript), where you can shave hours off your workflow by programming redundant editing or processing steps that can be automated and executed with a single keystroke. This could be used to rename all tracks, delete unused tracks, and bounce all tracks as audio files; or a keystroke to walk through an entire mixing process of 50 steps, down to the exact use of instrument templates, automations, and plugin settings. Your imagination is the limit in Reaper!

PROS

1	Reaper is extremely cost-effective: $60 for a personal-use license or $225 for a commercial license.
2	Reaper has a unique scripting language for automating and executing multiple commands in one keystroke.
3	Reaper has a fully-customizable interface.

CONS

1	Reaper's default graphical user interface (GUI) looks outdated.
2	MIDI editing in Reaper is unintuitive and has a steep learning curve for beginners.
3	No sample instruments are included in Reaper. Third-party plugins will be needed.

CONCLUSION

There are many other DAWs on the market, including **Studio One**, **Nuendo**, and **Reason** – I don't personally recommend these due to their lack of functionality when compared to the leading DAWs, but they certainly have cheaper price points for composers on a tight budget. Dedicated audio editors, including **Adobe Audition** and the free **Audacity**, are great for quick audio trims and conversions.

Many composers switch between multiple DAWs regularly. When choosing a DAW to start a project with, I focus on the creative flow needed to best serve the project. If I need to compose with MIDI on a Mac, I will use **Logic Pro**. If I need to score a film with a large orchestral template, I will use **Digital Performer**. If I need to compose immediately in a blank session, I will use **Cubase**. If I need to record or edit live audio, I will use **Pro Tools**. If I need to compose a video game loop, ambient music, or a dance track, I will use **Ableton Live**.

Master one DAW to increase your composing speed as quickly as possible.

With a world of options, what matters most is to *master one* DAW to increase your composing speed as quickly as possible. Only then should you consider adding more DAWs to your tool belt for more specific occasions.

Once you've chosen one DAW to master, it's also important to choose one notation software to master...

ACTION STEPS

1	What DAW am I most comfortable with?
2	Is another DAW more suitable for my creative workflow?
3	Should I consider using multiple DAWs to increase my composing quality and speed?

13

BEST NOTATION SOFTWARE FOR SHEET MUSIC?

Notation software is used to notate sheet music for the visual communication of musical ideas. At the core, sheet music is the heart of music composition. Much like an author who writes text to transmit his or her thoughts, sheet music conveys a composer's musical thoughts. Most often, sheet music is created for musicians to record a composer's track. Other times, composers use sheet music for analysis purposes or to generate a visual idea to transfer into a DAW for music production.

In any case, it's imperative for sheet music to be notated with impeccable clarity, intelligibility, and intentionality. Notation software speeds up the age-old handwritten approach and allows files to be shared quickly. With modern technology, orchestras can be hired remotely in other countries to record your sheet music by simply sending PDF parts and scores through email! Composers should make every attempt to transfer performance notes to sheet music for accurate recording, including the use of dynamics, phrase marks, tempo marks, etc. If musicians can't play your music as intended without your presence, then your sheet music isn't clear enough.

If musicians can't play your music as intended without your presence, then your sheet music isn't clear enough.

Finale, **Sibelius**, and **Dorico** are the three leading brands of notation software. Each is equally viable in the industry, but one may suit your creative workflow better than the others:

FINALE

If you can imagine it, you can notate it within **Finale** by Make Music. Due to its deep customization and numerous editing tools, Finale is heralded as the premier notation software for university music composition programs. Very much like Adobe Photoshop, Finale is a submenu program (menus within menus for pinpoint specificity). This program layout can be overwhelming at first open and difficult to master due to its large number of options. Finale is best suited for advanced composers specializing in detail-oriented music, who need to place unique symbols and instructions without restrictions. Finale has a steep learning curve but is beloved by the composers who have invested their time in learning its workflow.

SIBELIUS

Chosen by the majority of film composers, **Sibelius** by Avid is structured around being user-friendly. Instead of a submenu approach, Sibelius has one dedicated action for every notation input: one keystroke to add a note, add a dynamic, transpose notes, add a key signature, add an instrument, add lyrics, etc. Additionally, Sibelius' score layout is fully moveable – by simply clicking on any location, you can freely drag the score, simulating the ease of moving a real paper score. Likewise, score layouts are fully moveable by simply clicking and dragging to increase or decrease staff height, width, or the number of staves per page.

Sibelius' only true weakness is its lack of customization when composing complex music. It has a clunky symbol interface and poor ability to add custom instructions for musicians. Sibelius also requires downloading third-party plugins for advanced editing functions that are native to Finale.

Sibelius is ideal for composers who need to write professional-looking music quickly while allowing for multiple revisions. The film industry is notorious for asking composers to make quick, last-minute edits to music due to slight changes in scenes (every frame has to be accounted for!). Sibelius' ease-of-use is a wise choice for composers needing to make frequent changes.

DORICO

Dorico by Steinberg is the new kid on the block, marketing itself as *both* a DAW and notation software. Much like video editing software, the interface of Dorico is divided into multiple steps. This organization forces composers to create music in a preformatted manner: notation first (music composition), then DAW mixing (music production). In its current state, Dorico is best for beginners who have limited experience with notation software and DAWs. Advanced composers will find the limited features of Dorico to be frustrating when compared to other notation software or DAWs.

Dorico has yet to truly rise as a contender with Finale and Sibelius in the professional world due to its lack of identity and cohesion between its two steps. However, Dorico has recently shown great promise in its updates, bringing much-needed improvements to both steps. The market has yet to decide the best place for Dorico in a composer's workflow, but it is certainly worth trying to see if it benefits you!

HONORABLE MENTIONS

MuseScore and **NoteFlight** are both free notation software for Mac and PC. Both are extremely limited compared to Finale, Sibelius, and Dorico, but are great for beginners looking to create basic sheet music without advanced features. Thankfully, free 30-day trials are available for Finale, Sibelius, and Dorico, so you have the freedom to experiment with all three before choosing your favorite!

CONCLUSION

Once you've chosen one notation software to master, you can move on to upgrading the music gear in your studio...

ACTION STEPS

1	What notation software am I the most comfortable with?
2	Is another notation software more suitable for my creative workflow?
3	Should I consider using notation software more often when I compose?

14

BEST GEAR FOR A MUSIC STUDIO?

The following tools are my best recommendations for growing your music studio and business. While sample instruments and plugins are important (we'll focus on those next), most composers blow all their budget on those instead of investing in proper music gear and books to prepare their minds. I personally own and have used every product that I endorse. Because these resources have added so much value to me, I have become an affiliate partner with Amazon to share each at no additional cost to you.
Thanks for your support!

Most composers blow all their budget instead of investing in proper music gear and books to prepare their minds.

Best Music Gear Amazon List:
www.stevenmelin.com/musicgearlist

BOOKS ON MY BOOKSHELF

Books are not only the most affordable and accessible items in a music studio; they're also the most impactful. Here's a list of books that have made a significant impact on my composition career:

Start With Why by Simon Sinek is my top book recommendation for any creative seeking to start a business and build a brand. It has completely changed the way I do business – starting with my WHY instead of my WHO (target audience) or WHAT (products and services). This book is a must-read!

Jab, Jab, Jab, Right Hook by marketing guru Gary Vaynerchuck is the definitive guide for how to use each social media platform appropriately to maximize marketing results. Even though this book is dated (©2013), Gary's deep insight into using **Facebook, Twitter, Pinterest, Instagram,** and **Tumblr** to tell stories through micro-content is timeless and highly applicable to creatives working to establish a consistent and vibrant brand! This book has revolutionized the way I use social media to connect with my audience. I can't recommend it enough.

The 4-Hour Work-Week by Timothy Ferriss is my fastest-read book of all time. I believe I read all 400+ pages in just a few days. This gripping book is all about Defining your goals, Eliminating unproductive tasks from your life, Automating systems and outsourcing non-essential work, and Liberating yourself to achieve your dreams ("DEAL"). This book contains hundreds of useful, practical tips and advice from a business legend who lives what he preaches. This book has transformed my understanding that I am a business and not *just a composer*. This book has helped me exchange *busyness* for truly productive, meaningful work. Another must-read!

I've used ***The Complete Idiot's Guide to Music Composition*** to teach new composers the basics of music composition and production for the last several years. Don't be fooled by this book title! From cover to cover, this book is full of useful charts, tips, and shortcuts for writing great music fast. It teaches multiple methods for writing music, essential music theory, notation skills, scales and modes, advanced rhythms, musical tension and release, repetition and variations, writing outside basic key areas, songwriting, and more! This is essential reading for anyone who hasn't pursued a formal music degree.

A Composer's Guide to Game Music by Winifred Phillips is another amazing book on my bookshelf. As a current working composer for major video game titles, Phillips gives incredible insight into the business of the game industry. She describes how to become a professional composer, how to find work, how to write for every major game genre, and explores the intricacies of working with a development team.

If I could only choose one book for mixing, Mike Senior's *Mixing Secrets for the Small Studio* is it. This book explores the entire process of setting up a small home studio to maximize usability and to achieve the best possible mix on a budget. Senior then teaches the most efficient mixing workflow practices and how to best use each major plugin within a DAW (reverb, delay, stereo imaging, compression, etc.). This book isn't wide, but it's extremely deep.

Tonal Harmony: With An Introduction to Twentieth Century Music is the most widely trusted resource on the planet for teaching students the full range of music theory. This textbook is the source material for almost every high school and college music theory class and should be on the bookshelf of every composer. This book explores the entire history of written music with incredible detail and has visual and audio examples every step of the way. It also has benchmark exercises and review questions to test your skills throughout. While this book is most useful in a classroom setting, I actually bought it in high school and read the entire thing; it was so interesting and useful for me that I was able to pass the AP Music Theory exam (without taking the school class) and skip a music theory course in college. This book remains one of my most trusted resources, especially when I need a refresher on thick harmonic writing.

Samuel Adler's *The Study of Orchestration* is another massive textbook rich with visual and audio examples widely used in college music programs. More than any other resource, this book teaches the full depth of every classical orchestral instrument – its range, tessitura, best pairings with other orchestral instruments, notable uses in music history, best composition and notation practices, and a host of interesting facts about each instrument group. This book has opened my mind tremendously to the possibilities of the orchestra! It has significantly improved my ability to write more advanced music instead of relying on simple chord progressions and ostinatos. This is another must-have on a composer's bookshelf!

MUSIC GEAR IN MY STUDIO

There are thousands of music gear items to choose from on the market. This list contains my top recommendations for composers starting to build their studio.

I've recommended the *Yamaha P71 Digital Piano* to all my piano students because it's the most affordable weighted action 88-key keyboard on the market. While it doesn't boast the bells and whistles of other keyboards (hundreds of instruments sounds, LCD screen, transposition button, etc.), it compensates with a light-weight body for easy portability, loud on-board speakers, and a volume slider. It also has a USB cable port in the back for connecting to your computer and a headphone jack. Note that the included square-shaped sustain pedal in this package is complete garbage (poor response time and very awkward to use). Instead, I recommend the *Yamaha FC4* (see review below).

Any keyboard stand will do – my budget recommendation is the *On Stage Classic Single-X*. If you prefer to sit while playing versus standing, I recommend the budget-friendly foldable *On Stage Keyboard Bench* (benches are considerably better for your posture and back health than stools or chairs).

Every composer needs a MIDI controller to quickly record music in a DAW and to input data in notation software. My top requirements for any MIDI controller are that it must have semi-weighted keys (the best weight for recording both synths/electronic music and more sensitive instruments like orchestral and piano samples), a modulation wheel, a pitch bend wheel, and transposition up/down buttons. Any other features are bonuses (sliders, faders, drum pads, LCD screen, etc.). My top budget pick is the *M-Audio 49-Key Keystation Mk. II*. Right at $100, this MIDI controller has all these key features plus it doubles as an audio keyboard with a volume slider and 1/4" output! All MIDI keyboards have both MIDI and USB outputs, so you can easily connect this controller for all purposes. The reason I recommend the smaller 49-key model (versus the 61-key and 88-key) is for its small footprint on desks, easy portability, and cheaper price point. I have composed with MIDI controllers of all sizes and have found the 49-key to be the perfect size for composing in all environments due to its four-octave span (C to C) that can be easily transposed to other keys if needed.

If you find that you need to record with a full 88-keys, just record MIDI or audio from your full-size *Yamaha P71 Digital Piano* (see above review). In my opinion, purchasing an 88-key MIDI controller is a complete waste of money and space – it serves neither purpose (full mobile utility nor heavy-duty). If you must have five octaves instead of four, the 61-key Keystation works well, but isn't worth the extra $55 and larger footprint to me. Also note that if you purchase the Keystation bundle on Amazon, a copy of *Ableton Live Lite* is included! If budget isn't a concern, my favorite MIDI controller is the discontinued *M-Audio Axiom 49*, but its price is triple that of the Keystation (for good reason due to its included sliders, faders, transports, drum pads, and advanced programming functions). I find that these additional functions significantly speed up MIDI recording.

The **Yamaha FC4 Sustain Pedal** is my go-to pedal for all keyboards. I've tried all the cheaper brands and none of them have come close to the same response time and velocity control as this (due to its heavy base). Yes, this is a more expensive pedal, but it's designed for 10-15 years of heavy use. The cheap pedals wear considerably sooner and bring unnecessary frustration, including frequent polarity glitches and sticky pedals. Trust me on this one.

I never knew what great headphones could sound like until I tried a pair of **Audio-Technica ATH MX50 Headphones.** These are the best headphones on the market under $1000 (and it costs 1/5 less). You won't believe the crisp clarity and delicate bass-response on these headphones until you try them! Unlike the popular *Beats by Dre* headphones, the MX50 doesn't have a mid-range boost. These are flat headphones for mixing. They give you an incredibly accurate representation of your mix (for better or worse) and best of all, they're noise-cancelling *and* comfortable! I can wear these headphones for hours without my ears hurting or sweating. You may have noticed me wearing my white MX50's in my YouTube videos! As a bonus, these headphones also fold up nicely into a ball shape, come with a travel bag and multiple cord styles (short straight, long straight, and short coiled) – all which makes traveling super convenient! I take these headphones everywhere. Before the MX50, I used the KRK KNS-8400 headphones for years and thought they were the best headphones at this price point. I now consider that garbage! To me, the MX50 clarity is at least 5 times better!

The **RøDE NT1A** continues to be the best microphone you can purchase under $1,000 (and it costs 1/4 less). The NT1A's versatility at this price point is unmatched. Considered to be "the world's quietest studio microphone", you can record a gunshot one second then whisper the next and this mic will pick them both up without peaking (if you set your mic input level appropriately beforehand). I originally chose this condenser mic because I had heard from several musician friends that I could record any instrument with an extremely delicate response. As a multi-instrumentalist, I have found this to be incredibly true: from acoustic guitar to vocals (talking and singing) to hand percussion to violin to flutes, this mic has never disappointed with solo instrument recordings. I don't recommend it for group recordings because of its cardioid shape, but that's the only limitation I've found. The included pop-screen, shock mount, XLR cable, and mic carrying bag make this bundle on Amazon a no-brainer for any musician seeking to make a significant improvement in studio recording quality!

Note that in order to use this microphone, you will need an audio interface with phantom power (48V). My top recommendations are the *Focusrite Scarlett Solo*, *Scarlett 2i2*, and *Scarlett 18i20* (choose based on your budget and needs; see reviews below). In my experience, no other audio interface has the clarity, functionality, and simplicity of the *Focusrite Scarlett* series, especially at its incredible price point. The pre-amps in every Scarlett interface sound phenomenal and instantly make your recordings sound cleaner; and you can't ignore the beautiful red design of each box. Each box contains phantom power (48V) access with just the push of a button (necessary to power mics). For starting musicians, I recommend the *Scarlett 2i2* model because of its two inputs which allows you to leave two XLR or 1/4" cables connected (usually one for a vocal mic and one for an instrument like electric guitar, each of which you can conveniently set to a respective input volume level) and two outputs which allows you to connect two studio monitors for playback (essential for professional mixing). If your budget is tighter or you only plan to use headphones for playback (typical for mobile rigs), the *Scarlett Solo* should suffice. For musicians seeking optimum control and efficiency at an incredible price, the *Scarlett 18i20* is unbeatable. Boasting 18 inputs and 20 outputs, you'll always have the capacity for an army of instruments and mics handy when creativity strikes. I use the 18i20 so I can leave all my inputs set to my preferred volume levels for quick access. The 18i20 also includes a convenient visual Input Level Monitor that shows if a particular instrument is too soft or loud, Dim and Mute buttons for instant volume control (useful when switching between mic talkbacks and playback through studio monitors), and two headphone inputs – essential for recording music or podcasts with others in a live setting; this allows each musician to have individual volume control. If that's not enough, each of these audio interfaces is bundled on Amazon with *Pro Tools 12 First, Focusrite Creative Pack, Ableton Live Lite, Softube Time and Tone Bundle, Focusrite Red Plug-in Suite*, and 2GB of Loopmasters samples! This is a ridiculously good bundle. Don't pass it up.

KRK Rockit Studio Monitors are my favorite on the market. There's a reason why you see these iconic yellow tweeters in almost every music studio on the planet. The Rockit series monitors are heavy-duty (can be turned up to an insanely loud volume level – above 100dB, well beyond a movie theater) with a flat response, perfect for studio mixing. These monitors allow for every possible output format (RCA, TRS, and XLR), so they will work in every studio environment. There are multiple sizes available, but the ***Rockit 5's*** hit the best price point since they are bundled as a pair. The ***Rockit 6's*** only add one inch to the size, so the added volume and bass boost is unnecessary in my opinion for the additional $100. You can always expand to 2.1 later with a dedicated subwoofer or to 5.1 surround-sound with three additional Rockit 5's. With any dedicated studio monitors, you will need an audio interface (see *Focusrite Scarlett* review above). You will also need to isolate the studio monitors (you will get nasty buzz noises if you sit them on a desk) with stands or acoustic isolation pads. My budget recommendation is to buy two pairs of ***Auralex MoPAD Acoustic Isolation Pads***, one pair for each monitor to raise the monitors off your desk while conserving space. I have found these very useful in my small home studio setups.

A few years ago, I developed carpal tunnel symptoms in my wrist – no doubt a result of spending countless hours in front of my computer screen moving my mouse around in circles all day navigating large monitors. I used to consider myself a quick composer…until the pain was so great that I decided to make the switch to a trackball. Dozens of professional composer and producer friends recommended that I try the **Kensington Expert Trackball Mouse**. After a few days of learning how to use a trackball instead of a traditional mouse, my workflow speed increased significantly… easily double or triple the speed! Best of all, *no more wrist pain*. This trackball is simple and powerful: the trackball itself is slick and precise. You can adjust the sensitivity to your liking and enjoy precision both flicking your wrist across multiple monitors and while editing fine details. The scroll wheel makes web-browsing and screen-scrolling considerably quicker and the four shortcut buttons can be assigned to any key command or combo, making your favorite transport shortcuts a breeze. The Kensington Trackball comes in either a wired or wireless version. I prefer the wired model because of the cheaper price, and it doesn't require any battery changes. On a side-note: the included wrist cushion is useless. I found that it created *more* carpal tunnel issues…instead, I encourage picking up the inexpensive **ErgoBeads Wrist Cushion**.

If you plan to record an electric instrument such as an electric guitar or electric bass, you will need an Active Direct Box. My top recommendation is the **Behringer Ultra-DI DI100** for its straightforward functionality and incredible price. Simply plug in your 1/4" cable from your instrument into the DI box input and connect the DI box output to your audio interface; the result is a clean recording. Using a DI box protects your instrument and guarantees a fully-charged signal without having to increase your volume or create nasty instrument feedback noise.

Monster Cables are the best budget instrument cables on the market. Yes, there are less expensive cables available, but they usually break within a year of use or produce annoying hums and buzzes that leak into recordings. Monster has an incredible company policy – their lifetime guarantee promises that if one of their cables ever breaks from normal use, you can walk into any music store that sells their products (Guitar Center, Sam Ash, etc.) or contact Monster directly, and they will replace your broken cable at no charge! I strongly support companies with phenomenal customer service and Monster is well worth supporting.

CONCLUSION

Now that you've equipped your studio with the best music gear for your budget, you can move on to upgrading your sample instruments and plugins...

ACTION STEPS

1	What books have I recently read to grow my music business?
2	What is the most valuable gear in my music studio? Why?
3	What is one music gear investment I can make soon to add more value to my business?

15

BEST BUDGET SAMPLE INSTRUMENTS AND PLUGINS?

Now that you've established a foundation for your music studio and business, it's time to focus on building your sample instrument arsenal. There are hundreds of companies vying for your attention – many sample instruments and plugins are *good*, but only a handful are *great* among the sea of saturation.

Keep in mind that some of these companies offer educational discounts around 30% off and most give significant discounts on Cyber Monday week each year, up to 70% off! Waiting for these sales can go a long way, especially if you plan to buy multiple products at once. Also know that it may take several years to acquire a full setup. I suggest only purchasing what you *need* to compose for a *current* project. In many cases, you can add a *Music Gear* line item to your project budgets to afford the purchase of new libraries. I've done this many times to great effect, specifically when a client has requested a sound or instrument that I didn't have – I would just add the cost of that purchase to my bill in order to enhance the quality of my music and clients have happily paid for this every time.

Many sample instruments and plugins are good, but only a handful are great among the sea of saturation.

Here's my top list for any music composer on a budget seeking to assemble a balanced tool belt for composing any orchestral or electronic soundtrack:

SYNTHS

Native Instruments – Komplete 12 Ultimate ($1,199)

If I could only choose one purchase to last the rest of my career as a composer, it would be *Komplete 12 Ultimate* by Native Instruments. This insane bundle includes over 100 products and effects, 47,000 sounds, and over 600GB of library content! Most notable in the bundle is *Kontakt*, a sampler that allows you to create your own sample instruments from scratch. This one plugin has single-handedly changed the way I write music and develop my unique sonic fingerprint. Other staple instruments include *Massive*, *Absynth*, *FM8*, and *Reaktor* – all incredibly deep synthesizers that allow you to create an infinite supply of custom electronic sounds from the ground up. *Battery* is an amazingly useful drum machine and the gigantic number of orchestral instruments, rock instruments, ethnic instruments, and pianos in Komplete is truly all-inclusive. Specific to the Ultimate version are *Damage* (the premier industrial percussion engine), *Evolve* cinematic sounds bundle, *Symphony Essentials* (woodwinds, brass, strings), industry-leading piano samples *Una Corda* and *Alicia's Keys*, and so much more. When comparing versions, I don't recommend *Komplete 12 Select* due to the lack of full-version Kontakt (it only includes the free *Kontakt Player*) and its very mild selection of synths. When you purchase through Amazon, this Ultimate bundle includes a physical external hard drive to house all the samples, so this is a great deal to take advantage of.

Spectrasonics – Omnisphere 2 ($479)

Omnisphere is the industry-standard synth sampler. I've never seen a professional studio without it. I use Omnisphere in almost every track I write. Its extensive library contains thousands of useful presets – most notably Synth Pads, Synth Leads, and Keyboards of all kinds.

U-he: Zebra ($199)

Zebra is my favorite synthesizer, used exclusively by Hans Zimmer on many of his film scores. Urs Heckmann designed this synth to mimic analog modular synths. Zimmer's exact patches from the *Dark Knight* film series can be purchased in the **Dark Zebra** expansion.

BRASS

CineSamples: CineBrass Core ($399) / CineBrass Pro ($399)

There are numerous brass libraries on the market, but only one that I consider a true catch-all for all genres. CineSamples records all its orchestral libraries at the iconic Sony Pictures Scoring Stage in Los Angeles, so their libraries capture a distinct *Hollywood sound*. CineSamples splits all its orchestral articulations into two packs – **Core** and **Pro**. The Core versions contain all basic short and long articulations and the Pro features even more interesting play styles and European orchestral instruments. I consider both essential for a balanced orchestral library palette.

WOODWINDS

CineSamples: CineWinds Core ($349) / CineWinds Pro ($399)

CineWinds Core and *Pro* are the industry standards for woodwinds. Core includes the basic short and long articulations of the standard woodwind section (flutes, oboes, Bb clarinets, and bassoons). Pro features the extended woodwind section (alto and bass flutes, English horn, Eb clarinets) and multiple great non-orchestral woodwinds, such as the Uilleann pipes, whistles, and recorders.

8Dio: Claire Woodwinds Bundle ($973)

If you already own a woodwind ensemble library, picking up *Claire Woodwinds* will fill in your need for solo woodwinds – the heart of emotional orchestral music. This library contains seven deeply sampled legato solo woodwinds, including: Piccolo, Flute, Alto Flute, Oboe, English Horn, Bb Clarinet, and Bassoon. Each instrument is crafted for ultra-realistic performances, featuring patches for both slow and fast passages. These are the *most realistic* orchestral samples I have ever used. If the higher price is a concern, consider picking up any of the solo woodwinds individually for $138 each.

Berlin Woodwinds: Orchestral Tools ($495)

Berlin Woodwinds Orchestral Tools was the leading woodwind library for several years before *CineWinds*. Some composers still prefer it. It has a small roster, but each instrument is deeply sampled for detail. The full list includes Piccolo, Flute, Alto Flute, Oboe, English Horn, Bb Clarinet, and Bassoon. Flute Ensemble and Bb Clarinet Ensemble patches are also included.

STRINGS

Spitfire: Albion II Loegria ($449)

Spitfire has the highest-quality string libraries on the market, but they are also the most expensive by far. Spitfire is in the United Kingdom, so all their recordings have a distinct *British film sound*. *Albion II Loegria* is a collection of soft British orchestral strings, brass, and woodwinds with extended techniques. I use the flautando strings (high, flute-like violins) and euphoniums (soft British horns) in almost every soundtrack. No other library captures this mellow pianissimo tone so beautifully.

8Dio: Adagietto Strings ($119)

Adagietto Strings is the most price-sensitive string collection on the market. Its roster is simple with only 4 instruments: Violin, Viola, Cello, and Double Bass. Each instrument is deeply sampled with the most realistic legato, staccato, spiccato, tremolo, and pizzicato patches. You won't find extended techniques here (trills, glissandos, col legno, etc.), but when combined with *Albion II Loegria*, this is a powerhouse budget combo.

PERCUSSION

Impact Soundworks: Rhapsody Orchestral Percussion ($199)
Rhapsody Orchestral Percussion is a one-stop product for all orchestral percussion essentials. This pack includes 50 traditional and extended percussion instruments recorded through three mic positions. These clean recordings are neither clinically dry nor overly epic. This flexible library is designed for the full range of scoring – from intimate cues to dramatic and bombastic.

Heavyocity: Damage ($299)
When you need edgy, modern percussion for hybrid scores, *Damage* is the solution. This pack includes both loop and kits classified into four styles: Epic Organic, Epic Tech, Industrial Electronic, and Mangled Pop. My most-used patches are the epic Armageddon Ensemble and metallic Dumpster, highly useful when scoring movie trailers and television commercials.

CHOIR

SoundIron: Requiem Light ($199)
There are numerous choir libraries on the market, but *Requiem Light* is my top budget recommendation. It contains full choir, male choir, female choir, and soloists with legato vowels, staccato shouts, and a phrase builder. Even though this library is slightly dated, *Requiem Light* remains my favorite sample choir in any epic orchestral scoring situation. Its older brother *Requiem Professional* by 8Dio contains more patches, but at the steeper price point of $548.

Spitfire Labs: Eric Whitacre Choir (free)

This choir only features one simple *Ooo* articulation, but this instrument is too good to be free. This choir is at home in any soft, ambient orchestral track.

ETHNIC / WORLD

UVI: World Suite ($299)

With over 320 ethnic instruments (50,000 samples) and 8,000 loops and phrases, this collection of traditional instruments from around the globe is essential. This one suite fills in the gap where **Komplete** and all the above orchestral libraries fall short. World music is often overlooked by composers but is a crucial piece for crafting modern soundtracks for international markets. This pack features instrument categories: Africa, Asia, Australia, Celtic, Eastern Europe, India, Indonesia, Middle East, Occidental, South America, Spanish Gypsy, and West Indies.

CHIPTUNE

DefleMask (free)

If you're seeking to create authentic retro video game music, *DefleMask* is the best tracker available. Unlike DAWs, trackers notate music through hexadecimal code and require a bit of learning. The result is well worth the effort though. *DefleMask* allows you to compose chiptunes for SEGA Genesis, SEGA Master System, Nintendo Game Boy, NEC PC-Engine, Nintendo NES, Commodore 64, and Arcade System – all with the same coding language. When you finish a track, you can export it as a WAV (to be used in a game engine) or a VGM/MMF/ROM to port it directly into the original console hardware. Best of all, *Deflemask* is free and available on both PC and Mac. *FamiTracker* is another great free tracker but doesn't support as many game consoles and is only for PC.

Plogue: Chipsounds ($95)

If you plan to compose video game music in a DAW, *Chipsounds* is a must-have. Thankfully, traditional 8Bit channels (pulse wave, triangle wave, and white noise) are easy to emulate freely in most default DAW synths. However, when you decide to dive deeper into recreating vintage sounds such as old arcade chips, Atari 2600, Commodore 64, etc., your options are to compose in a tracker, acquire the actual hardware, or use *Chipsounds* in a DAW. As much as I enjoy composing in trackers, there are times when I need the flexibility of composing MIDI in a DAW with the exact retro sounds.

Impact Soundworks: Super Audio Boy (free)

Super Audio Boy is another great free tool for quickly composing 8Bit chiptunes. This is my go-to plugin for writing Nintendo NES and Game Boy music in a DAW. I enjoy its clean interface that already contains pulse waves separated by pulse width, drum samples, and SFX – all designed specifically for NES and Game Boy music. Its big brother *Super Audio Cart ($149)* contains patches for Atari 2600, Commodore 64, Nintendo NES, Nintendo Famicom, Nintendo Game Boy, Super Nintendo, SEGA Master System, and SEGA Genesis.

It Might Get Loud Productions: Koji Keyboard ($46)

The 16Bit *Super Nintendo sound* is characterized by highly-compressed samples. Most SNES composers created their own samples by compressing sounds from Yamaha keyboards into small enough sizes to fit on the limited game cartridge memory – the result was a unique instrument palette for each game. Thankfully, It Might Get Loud Productions has done this sampling and compression process with the ***Koji Keyboard***. This simple library includes 57 instruments, all crafted for instant composing out-of-the-box. I have found the *Koji Keyboard* to be a vital addition to my 16Bit Super Nintendo template.

BOUTIQUE

Embertone / Bolder Sounds

New sample instrument companies enter the global market every year and many of the smaller teams produce unique content at an impressively low cost! Some of my personal favorites include the Embertone ***Chapman Trumpet*** and Bolder Sounds ***Harmonica***.

PIANO

Spectrasonics – Keyscape ($399)

Keyscape is the industry-standard keyboard sampler. This massive collection features 36 keyboard models, including the famous Yamaha C7 grand, Rhodes electric pianos, Wurlitzers, Planets, Clavichord, and many more. I use the pianos in this library on almost every project. As a bonus, all Keyscape patches can be loaded directly into Omnisphere to create versatile multis.

Spitfire Labs: Soft Piano (free)

This felt piano is extremely soft and will need to be compressed or doubled with another piano to be audible in your mix, but this is the most beautiful, intimate piano sample I have every used…and it's free! This is an ideal piano sample for soft film scenes. Spitfire Labs also offers other free instruments that are well-worth downloading.

MIXING

FabFilter / Waves / 2CAudio / iZotope

The best mixers in the world use the least number of plugins. Yet, there are thousands of products on the market to choose from, most of which sell you the idea that you need large bundles of plugins to achieve a great mix. Instead, I encourage you to invest in a small number of high-quality mixing plugins and learn to use each well. Every composer needs a quality equalizer (EQ), compressor, reverb, delay, limiter, ultramaximizer, and mastering suite. You will find all these with FabFilter *Pro-Q* and *Pro-C*, Waves *Gold* or *Silver* bundle, 2CAudio *2CAether*, and iZotope *Ozone 8 Advanced*. Only after acquiring these basic mixing essentials should you consider adding more experimental plugins to your palette.

ACTION STEPS

1	What are the most valuable sample instruments in my music studio? Why?
2	When was the last time I upgraded my sample instruments or plugins to have a higher quality sound?
3	What is one sample instrument or plugin investment I can make soon to add more value to my business?

SECTION SUMMARY

If you've read *PART 4: Best Tools for Composing* and followed the Action Steps, then you've successfully chosen one DAW and one notation software to master and have acquired the most effective hardware and software for your studio.

Your music business is now equipped with the essential tools and is ready to scale. Move on to *PART 5: Music Business Growth*.

MUSIC BUSINESS GROWTH

16

WORK HABITS OF SUCCESSFUL MUSIC COMPOSERS?

Running a successful music business involves much more than composing music. Without healthy work habits, you will burnout, become uninspired, and dislike your career. Here are five work habits to establish a successful career as a music composer:

1. DAILY DEEP WORK

Deep Work is focused work without distractions. Deep Work is usually considered three or more hours of time dedicated to one task and multiple periods of Deep Work in a week is crucial for developing a successful work week. This kind of work has an exponential return on time invested when compared with common smaller time periods spread across multiple tasks. Deep Work will rarely occur naturally in our busy culture – it must be intentionally set aside.

> **Without healthy work habits, you will burnout, become uninspired, and dislike your career.**

2. MAINTAIN ALL RIGHTS TO MUSIC

Most composers neglect music rights discussions because they consider contracts to be too complicated or time-consuming. This neglect usually results in sticky agreements or lack of clarity about music rights. If you're composing for an indie project that is paying less than $20,000, you should never trade your music rights. The purpose of owning 100% of your music rights is so you can sell your music in other arenas later, such as a soundtrack or streaming services. Projects with low compensation (less than $1,000) should never be given exclusive rights to the music. *Exclusive* rights allow a company full usage of the music, in exclusive association with their brand. *Non-exclusive* rights allow the composer to resell and relicense the music to other buyers for use in other projects. Most development teams desire exclusive rights to your music to establish their own sonic identity, but you should charge a premium for this customization.

If you're scoring music for a large, premium project paying over $20,000, you should consider exchanging your music rights for the higher pay. Larger companies usually have tight control over their Intellectual Property (IP) and require both exclusivity and all rights to your music – this is considered a *Work for Hire* agreement. Since these premium projects are less frequent than the smaller ones, I encourage you to retain your rights whenever possible. You never know when the next indie project you score will become a smash hit...your soundtrack sales will thank you when that happens. Even if you never experience that level of spontaneity, soundtrack sales and stream revenue usually exceed the commission of scoring the soundtrack itself.

3. BE PLEASANT TO WORK WITH

Successful projects are a result of tightly-knit creative teams. If there is one weak link or rotten attitude in the team, the entire project suffers. Being a music composer within a team dynamic has far less to do with your talent level or production skills and more to do with the energy you bring to the team. If you're a mediocre composer, but deliver music before deadlines, encourage other team members, and work diligently without needing any reminders, you are *valuable* to the team. You will attract more jobs by being a team player. On the contrary, if you're an incredibly talented composer, but are a pain to work with, your name will spread quickly within our tiny industry and you will likely be blacklisted. Bad attitudes repel job opportunities. When you're part of a team, you are working towards the vision of the team, never your own vision.

4. SET REALISTIC DEADLINES

Meeting deadlines is a vital skill for building trust within a team and paving a long-term successful career. Project deadlines wait for no one, so it's wise to expect unexpected life events. We certainly can't know what the future holds, so we should reduce risk however possible when planning our calendars. One of my practices is to schedule all project deadlines 1.5 times later than my intentions. If I'm scoring five tracks for a project and I expect to finish within three weeks, I will negotiate a deadline of five weeks to account for any complications, life events, or additional project requests and communications. This buffer allows me to breathe, knowing that I have the freedom to make mistakes. No one can perform at full efficiency every work day. There will be times that I compose slower than anticipated. There will be times that I'm utterly uninspired to compose. There will be family emergencies, last-minute invitations to important events, and in my case as a foster parent – constant rescheduling within my calendar. Why live a stressed and rushed life? You can prevent this (and consequently prevent dropping the ball) by simply expanding your deadlines.

Additionally, whenever I agree to a deadline with a client, I schedule my own internal deadlines a week or two sooner. In the best-case scenario, this allows me to turn in work early or get feedback from trusted friends before submitting. Worst-case scenario, I meet all deadlines and my integrity is unscathed, regardless of how many hardships I had to overcome to complete the project on time. In every project, my goal is to under-promise and over-deliver.

5. ALWAYS BE LEARNING

The most successful people in the world are lifelong learners. They read books every day. They practice every day. They serve others every day. They intentionally make every day count.

As a composer, it's easy to get in a rut and develop debilitating Creative Burnout (addressed in a future chapter). Surrounding yourself with inspiration and environments for learning causes healthy growth. Integrating regular learning into your daily work life will develop great success as you continue to grow.

CONCLUSION

Once you've established these healthy work habits, you're ready to develop business growth habits…

ACTION STEPS

1	What is my strongest work habit today?
2	What is my weakest work habit today?
3	What is one work habit that I can add or improve today?

17

DEVELOPING BUSINESS GROWTH HABITS?

Your time matters as a music composer. If you want to be efficient with your time and build long-lasting relationships with clients, it's imperative to establish healthy daily habits. Here are five routines that have changed my career:

1. READ NON-FICTION BOOKS

Yes, we live in a digital age. But when was the last time you cracked open a physical book and read it cover-to-cover? If you do nothing else on this list, my top encouragement is for you to establish a daily habit of reading non-fiction books. If you have the extra time, enjoy fiction books on the side – they're great for expanding our imaginations and entertainment – but non-fiction books strengthen our weaknesses, offer fresh perspectives, and answer questions we haven't asked yet. No other activity in life offers the same rich return on investment (ROI) for the small amount of time and energy given. I recommend setting aside 30 minutes to an hour daily. It will change your life.

"You are the same today you'll be in five years except for two things: the people you meet and the books you read."

– Charlie Jones

2. PRACTICE YOUR CRAFT

If you're a composer, compose music every day. If you're an author, write every day. If you're a musician, play your instrument every day. The amount doesn't matter. Just do it.

Writer's Block is a real condition, but it's also a choice. Those who practice every day may not enjoy it every time, but they are improving. Nothing can replace time and experience. As Thomas Edison taught us, there is value in learning 1,000 ways how *not* to make a light bulb. I guarantee he knew exactly how to make a light bulb *every time* after that.

Nothing can replace time and experience.

"Practice does not make perfect – it makes permanent."
– Alexander Libermann

3. ESTABLISH A CONSISTENT SCHEDULE

Consistency is everything. Do you want to maximize your workflow? Schedule your life to function as you function best. Some people (I included) tackle creative endeavors best in the morning and admin work best during the afternoon slump. Others have more energy in the afternoon and prefer to tackle composition then. Introverts prefer solo work in the morning to be recharged so they can energetically meet with others and invest in relationships in the afternoon. Extroverts desire personal interactions immediately in the morning to be recharged to tackle personal pursuits later in the day. However you function best, establish a healthy rhythm in your calendar.

It's also important to be flexible with your schedule to accommodate unexpected events and circumstances. If you work with an attitude that no one is an inconvenience, you'll never be interrupted again.

Maintain a consistent schedule as much as possible but avoid rigidity. Success isn't always about greatness. It's about *consistency*.

"Consistent hard work leads to success. Greatness will come."

– Dwayne Johnson

4. INTERACT WITH YOUR TRIBE

One of the best ways to stay current and forward-thinking is to daily commune with others in your tribe. No one person has it all figured out. We need each other to succeed.

Technology has blessed us with countless avenues to interact with others: **Facebook, Instagram, Twitter, YouTube,** forums, etc. Find the "watering hole" where your tribe hangs out. Ask questions and join conversations. Most importantly, *listen*. Perhaps one of the places for you to interact is the private Sonic Storytellers Facebook Group I co-lead.

"If you are the smartest person in the room, then you are in the wrong room."

– Confucius

5. RESEARCH ON THE GO

Imagine a film director or game developer approaching you and describing their ideal sound for their latest story – how valuable would it be if you had a database where after searching for one or two keywords (adjectives used directly by the creator, such as *cheerful, foreboding, warm*, etc.), a list of tracks appears with exact instrumentations used to achieve these moods with track URLs? As a bonus, each of these tracks is music that you already *love listening to*. This is the power of consistent, quality research.

How do you assemble a database with this power? Every day, at the same consistent time, listen to 5 new music tracks *on the go* – this can be while checking emails, reading articles, exercising, getting ready in the morning, eating meals, driving, etc. Not only will this inspire you every day, but by keeping an organized database, you will prepare yourself to write better music with greater efficiency (*less revisions*). I keep a spreadsheet with Excel easily accessible from my desktop. You may find this database creation easier on the go by using Notes, Evernote, or Google Docs from your mobile devices.

While listening to new music tracks, jot down the date, album, track number, track title, URL source, instrumentation choices that stand out, and the resulting mood. Even if you only do this for 6 days, you'll already have 30 diverse examples. Imagine doing this for a month (120) or a year (1,560). That's a serious database.

This same concept applies for all media, not just music – watching TV shows and movies, playing video games, reading screenplays, etc. You're already consuming media daily – why not make it useful for your business growth? Make your research concrete and useful by keeping records. Daily research the media that you desire to work on and you'll be an expert in your field in no time.

"Research is formalized curiosity. It is poking and prying with a purpose."
– Zora Neale Hurston

CONCLUSION

Once you've developed these five business growth habits, you're ready to move on to *Chapter 19: Networking and Gaining Repeat Clients*; or you may first need to learn how to deal with Creative Burnout…

ACTION STEPS

1	What is my strongest business habit today?
2	What is my weakest business habit today?
3	What is one business habit that I can add or improve today?

18

DEALING WITH CREATIVE BURNOUT?

As composers, we have a natural challenge for managing our energy levels and time. As a result, we tend to experience Creative Burnout, a condition that paralyzes both our artistry and business growth. Creative Burnout manifests itself in two frustrating ways:

1. *Depleted Willpower*: lacking the mental or emotional strength to work on a creative project. In these moments, we would rather do *anything else* besides work on a project.

2. *Writer's Block*: lacking creative ideas, even though energy and passion are full. This is discouraging because we're not happy with anything that we write.

Composers most commonly experience Creative Burnout immediately after finishing a large project, typically a feature film or video game soundtrack, where over 30 minutes of music is required in a short period of time. Pouring out our energy at such a high capacity leads to significant drainage that can easily damage our lives. If left unchecked, Creative Burnout leads to devastating, career-ending questions: *Should I even be a composer? Am I even skilled at my craft? Does anyone like what I create?*

Understanding how to prevent Creative Burnout and how to escape it if it creeps into our lives is of paramount importance for every composer.

HOW TO PREVENT CREATIVE BURNOUT

Inspiration prevents Creative Burnout. Consistently consuming content that enlightens you is key for maintaining inspiration and staying current. As a music composer, ask yourself "What media inspires me?" For many of us, listening to new music on **Spotify**, **Apple Music**, or **YouTube** will suffice. For others, watching new TV shows and movies or playing video games will inspire. Whatever your muse, habitually include it in your life to stay inspired.

Inspiration prevents Creative Burnout.

Just as muscles in the body need to be maintained, creativity must be engaged to remain healthy. If creativity is unused, it will shrink. If it is overused, it will be injured and will require a lengthy recovery time. Rest is a key component for achieving balance. I personally work five days a week, Monday through Friday, and rest my creativity on the weekends to enter the following week recharged. I also take breaks throughout my work days – to eat lunch, to enjoy a TV show or video game, to walk around outside, to go on a date with my wife, to meet with a friend, etc. These breaks help support a constant flow of creativity, especially when they are consistent.

HOW TO ESCAPE CREATIVE BURNOUT

If you find yourself stuck in Creative Burnout, it's important to act as soon as possible. Sometimes all we need to break out of Creative Burnout is to refresh our perspective. Simply switching to a different project can refresh our mind. I make a habit of cycling between 2-3 projects every week – some are products in production and others are custom scoring gigs for clients. If I feel tired from composing large amounts of music, I can both recharge and remain productive by working on music products, such as courses, podcast episodes, or blog articles.

If you feel completely unmotivated to do *any* productive work in your studio, take a break for a few hours and return refreshed. Some ideas include spending time outside, engaging in physical activity, meeting with a friend, or going out for an errand. Do whatever you can to leave your home and connect with the world around you. In extreme cases of Creative Burnout, take several days off – perhaps even a week or two – to recover away from your studio. Twice a year, my wife and I plan a one-week vacation to recharge away from home without our children. These breaks clear my mind and provide deep renewal.

CONCLUSION

Now that you're equipped to prevent or escape Creative Burnout, you're ready to learn how to network and gain repeat clients...

ACTION STEPS

1	Have I ever dealt with Creative Burnout? If so, how did I escape it?
2	What would cause me to fall into Creative Burnout?
3	What is one way that I can prevent Creative Burnout today?

19

NETWORKING AND GAINING REPEAT CLIENTS?

If you're seeking more work, networking is an essential component of any freelance industry. In the business world, we often throw around the word *networking* to mean the awkward process of meeting strangers at conferences or shaking hands at events, but at the core, networking is about establishing *relationships* with clients that last a lifetime. Maintaining lifetime, repeat clients is a result of bringing *value* to your target audience. If you can narrow down your target audience to a small, niche audience, they will gladly pay for your solution to their problem; your solution has greater value to them than their money. After all, they're going to spend that money on something else if not on you.

> **Maintaining lifetime, repeat clients is a result of bringing value to your target audience.**

Networking should always start from your local area and branch outwards. Most composers confuse this order by starting at the macro level – contacting big corporations, big game developers, and big film directors, but this is the fastest route to discouragement and rejection. When you start networking with your local area, you bypass competition. By interacting directly with people within your first-degree and second-degree network (personal friends or friends of friends), you will land jobs significantly faster, especially in our digital age where face-to-face interactions have deep impressions. Living locally to new contacts makes it easy and convenient to share a meal, invite each other to events, and quickly chat about jobs as they arise. Local networking opportunities range wildly, from city events, creator meet-ups, game jams, and everything in-between. Many film and video game organizations already have regular meetings, including **Grammy Pro**, **Game Audio Network Guild (GANG)**, and **International Game Developers Association (IGDA)**. If there are no relevant organizations in your area, consider starting your own chapter or using social media to launch a meet-up at your local coffee shop, library, or park. Kickstart your career by being the big fish in your local small pond.

Once you've begun to exhaust your local area, invest time and energy in regional events. These include conferences, university master classes, one-day workshops, etc. – all great opportunities to spend time directly with your target audience. If you're a video game composer, look for game developer conferences. If you're a film composer, look for filmmaker workshops.

On a global level, the internet provides an incredible means for communicating with audiences around the world. There are countless communities and platforms to invest your time and energy into. Due to this overwhelming amount of opportunity, composers are often paralyzed when deciding where to invest their time and energy. To help narrow it down, I suggest focusing on which platforms provide the greatest amount of *attention* for your effort. **Twitter** and **Tumblr**, for example, are not what they once were. While both platforms still exist, neither yields any worthwhile attention compared to **Facebook**, **Instagram**, and **YouTube** – the holy trinity of social media that dominates the internet. According to social media marketing expert Gary Vaynerchuck, if your brand is not on one of these three platforms, you are irrelevant. The internet provides so many opportunities for music composition jobs, but your success landing jobs is fully determined by how you position yourself to receive work.

My first few custom scoring opportunities were all from local relationships in Atlanta, Georgia. Future gigs resulted from online relationships built over time through establishing authority on social media. Most of my career has been built on only a handful of repeat clients. I find it curious that my highest paid and most frequent work is now also local in Atlanta. I contribute this to the personal relationships I've built over time – my work quality has increased, as has theirs, and we have a thriving symbiotic business relationship. My clients earn more revenue with each new project and they're happy to increase my rates every time. Repeat clients are fun to work with, easy to communicate with, and are the backbone of any successful career.

CONCLUSION

Now that you know how to network and establish repeat clients, you're ready to move on to *PART 6: Music Business Strategies*. Or perhaps you'd first like to consider becoming an intern for a music composer or hiring an assistant to scale faster...

ACTION STEPS

1	How effective are my networking habits currently?
2	What is one action I can take today to improve my networking skills?
3	How can I retain work from previous clients?

20

HOW VALUABLE ARE COMPOSER INTERNSHIPS?

Does an internship or assistantship with an established music composer have an impact on your career? Maybe. Your career path is unique, as is mine. No one path can be replicated, but I hope that by sharing insights from my experiences, you may receive more clarity into the next steps of your journey. Whether or not you pursue an internship or assistantship will determine greatly upon your past experiences, current life situation, and future goals. Working with another composer is *not* for everybody. Many composers have paved their own career success without the help of other composers; however, those who intern usually fast-track the advancement of their career growth.

> **Those who intern usually fast-track the advancement of their career growth.**

If you're in your early 20's, not in school, not married, and without kids – you're an ideal candidate to be an intern or assistant for a composer. Your life is far less complicated than most and you have a level of flexibility that will ensure a positive experience working in a studio environment. You have a large amount of time to sacrifice, little concern for expenses, and energy to invest. Internships and assistantships usually pay very little (if at all), so I only advise seeking one out if you believe that the learning experience will have a direct impact on both your immediate and long-term business success.

Both internships and assistantships run the gambit of expectations from errand-running to administrative organization, music editing, and additional music work.

Intern positions are usually unpaid and short-term, based around temporary projects or seasons. Most Hollywood composers have an annual intern position that rotates every year. These composer teams receive hundreds of applications throughout the year and positions are typically given to recent Music Composition graduates from top colleges and universities. These positions are less hands-on but provide opportunities to *be in the room* while composers work. Exceptional interns are usually asked to become assistants after a full term; but they must be truly exceptional – adding value to the team that far exceeds the expectations.

Assistant positions are usually long-term and are extremely difficult to obtain. These positions are paid, competitive, and deeply valuable. Assistants significantly aid composers – they ensure that composers meet all deadlines, produce maximum quality work, and always remain organized. The key role of an assistant is *not* to be a co-composer, but to *equip* the composer to succeed every day.

In my early career, I had the pleasure of working with three Hollywood composers – two internships and one assistantship. As part of my final semester in Los Angeles during my MFA Music Composition for the Screen degree at Columbia College Chicago (CCC), I interned with documentary and film composer Joel Goodman (*Being Elmo*, *American Experience*). During my internship, I primarily helped organize his extensive music databases. This taught me how to organize my own music databases and how to work with a team of assistants. During the same time period, I reached out to video game and film composer Garry Schyman (*Middle-earth: Shadow of Mordor*, *Bioshock*) and he welcomed me to his studio to assist with sample instrument creation. Working hands-on with Garry, I learned how to create a massive DAW orchestral template and work with a live orchestra.

After graduating from CCC, composer Penka Kouneva (*The Mummy* VR game, *Prince of Persia: The Forgotten Sands*) hired me to assist remotely as I moved to Atlanta, Georgia. For a year I assisted Penka with research, data collection, and client communications; these have proven to be invaluable skills for my own business. This assistantship was a great source of supplemental income while building my own composition career.

Most composers are unaware of remote internship and assistantship opportunities – with technology advancements, there is no barrier to sharing data, DAW sessions, music resources, etc. For composers without the opportunity to travel to Los Angeles or New York, working remotely can provide valuable connections and relationships to further your career.

Should you seek out an internship or assistantship? If you can, yes. Many of you are not in a position to. I currently have four children and I couldn't provide for my family with the pay cut and time sacrifice of assisting. However, many of you *can* and will experience a boost to your career. Internships and assistantships are best found by starting locally. Local connections are always the most powerful and will lead to the most practical opportunities. I recommend contacting your local composers and inviting them to coffee or lunch. Ask questions to learn more about their business and offer ways to offload their stress. Find creative solutions to their problems and you will likely invent a job for yourself.

Whether or not you're able to seek out an internship or assistantship, I highly advise seeking out composer mentorships whenever possible. *Mentorships* are opportunities to have extended personal chats with your heroes to learn their stories, work habits, failures, and recommendations. Most composers are more accessible than you may think – reaching out to them (or their assistants) by email or phone is usually enough to start a conversation. If you're local, visiting composers in their studio can provide an opportunity to learn about their workflow, studio setup, and daily routines. **Skype** chats are also valuable for those out of distance. Attending industry events and conferences is an amazing way to start initial conversations with composers that can lead to future mentorships. I've enjoyed mentorships with industry pros Grant Kirkhope (*Banjo Kazooie, GoldenEye 007*), Jason Graves (*Tomb Raider, Dead Space*), and Austin Wintory (*The Banner Saga, Journey*). Learning from industry leaders has greatly accelerated my career growth.

CONCLUSION

Once you've determined the value of becoming a music composer intern or assistant, it's time to pursue that route or skip to *PART 6: Music Business Strategies*. Or perhaps you'd first like to consider hiring an assistant to scale faster...

ACTION STEPS

1	Would an internship or assistantship be valuable for my career? Why?
2	How do I plan to continue my education throughout my career?
3	What is one action I can take today to begin a composer mentorship?

21

HOW VALUABLE IS AN ASSISTANT?

If you're earning *any* amount of consistent monthly income as a music composer, you should outsource some of your tasks! As long as you spend less money than you earn, you'll grow your business while saving countless hours.

True business growth occurs when you stop trading time for dollars. The only way to free up time is to automate tasks that can be carried out by systems – this includes creating products and selling them on marketplaces. For example, instead of requiring an interested client to contact you through email and replying with a manual invoice, upload your music to a marketplace and let that system sell, invoice, distribute, and collect payments for you. Or instead of teaching one student at a time and earning an hourly rate, create a course that can be sold thousands of times after only 50 hours invested in its creation – this is a significant multiplier. Systems save you time, which save you money – even if this costs you a little money, time, or sales commission upfront.

> **If someone else can do it, hire it out.**

All other tasks that can be completed by *anyone but yourself* should be. If someone else can do it, hire it out. No one is a master of all skills, but you need to be a master of one. If you're not a master of a skill, hire someone who is. Once your schedule is freed up to focus on what you're *best* at, you will excel and earn more income as a result! Once you establish your monthly income goal, setup systems that sell your products, and delegate replicable tasks to assistants, you'll have the freedom to charge a premium price for your specialized skillset. After all, you have business expenses to cover and a profit to maintain.

Perhaps the best benefit of hiring an assistant is the preceding elimination of all unnecessary and unproductive tasks from our work routine. There's something powerful about investing money – we stop and think to ensure that all money spent will result in a positive outcome. This causes us to reduce risks and make wiser decisions. In some cases, it requires us to completely scrap a project that we once considered a good idea.

I've personally hired several assistants in recent years to aid with social media, marketing, artwork, data management, product assembly, audio editing, blog writing, podcast production, and more. I have yet to hire a permanent assistant but have experienced significant return on my short-term project investments and plan to continue doing so in the future as needs arise. I earn considerably more than I spend every time.

When hiring an assistant, it's important to consider that they can't read your mind. If you have a process or system for a task, it's essential for you to have a documented step-by-step outline to provide to your assistant. This is the most effective communication to replicate high-quality results as if you're completing the task yourself.

There are many great books on this subject. *The 4-Hour Workweek* by Timothy Ferriss, mentioned in an earlier chapter, has been a best-selling business book for decades. It poses the questions: What if you could only work four hours per week? How would you spend your time? What are the most essential tasks that *only you* can accomplish? At the core of your business, there should be one or two tasks that only you can do. This book arrested me when I first read it because at that time, I had spent about five years composing music professionally, but hadn't taken the Music Business pillar seriously. I had been wearing all the hats in my business – music composition, production, editing, mixing, invoicing, admin work, communications…about 20 weekly roles! Running a business under such weight causes stress and the inability to devote attention to the quality of any one task. Being pulled in so many directions prevents focus and Deep Work. This is particularly frustrating for composers, because they usually don't have the funds to hire other people at the start. What if you could only work four hours a week? Would you make wiser decisions about your time? Wouldn't you find a way to maximize those hours by focusing on what you love doing the most?

Start With Why by Simon Sinek is another fantastic book on this subject, also cited in an earlier chapter. This book challenges you to strip your business down to the core of Why you have a business in the first place. Then you can figure out your What (products and services) and How you plan to offer them. This took a lot of soul-searching for me. I'm capable of doing a lot of things in my business: I can produce music, I can write blogs, I can film videos, I can record podcasts, I can create courses…there are unlimited ways to fill up my schedule and to stay busy, but how many of these tasks move the needle forward in my business? If you tally up the hours required to accomplish all these tasks, they equal more hours than a full-time job. You can't do it all. That's unrealistic and unsustainable. This is the core root of Creative Burnout. It's hard to do anything with extreme excellence when you're constantly fighting to prioritize tasks.

The purpose of an assistant is to complete all the tasks that aren't your core strengths. This is how you scale your business. Your time is valuable. As the owner of your business, your time is the most valuable of anyone in your company. Stop wasting time on tasks that earn less dollars than your time is worth.

Let's consider a blog article – on average, it takes me two or three hours to write an article. Through affiliate marketing, a blog article may earn $50 to $100 over the course of a month – this is only about $3 earned per working hour! Contrast this with composing music, my core strength. On average, I earn $200 to $400 per hour composing. This is a significant difference. In this situation, I would much rather spend $20 an hour to hire an assistant to write the blog article, costing around $60, versus the opportunity cost of hundreds or even thousands from spending my time focusing on writing a blog instead of music. As a bonus, the blog article written by an expert will likely be at a higher quality level than anything I could create. This same concept can be applied to web design, social media, marketing, data organization, project creation, artwork, and so many other tasks that composers tend to *burn money* on while focusing on the secondary tasks of their business.

If you feel bogged down in your business and wonder why it isn't growing at the rate you had hoped, it's likely because you aren't investing in the weaknesses of your business. If you're earning money in your craft right now on *any* consistent basis, even if it's only $100 per month, you can afford an assistant in some capacity. Here are three solutions that I have found for hiring assistants:

1. UPWORK

Upwork is a freelance website for hiring assistants on a project or recurring basis. Much like eBay or Craigslist, it's an open marketplace that should be treated with caution. There are many great opportunities for hiring quality assistants, but my recommendation is to only pursue short, temporary hires to reduce risk. One of the benefits to an open and global marketplace is easy access to low-cost services from countries with lower rate exchanges, such as the Philippines, which is known for its high-quality workers that charge only a few dollars per hour. This is a great option when you only have a small budget to spend on outsourcing simple, repeatable tasks such as social media, marketing, video editing, etc. – anything that doesn't rely heavily on native English skills. If you choose to go this route, I highly recommend creating a step-by-step instruction list for each task to reduce errors and increase accuracy.

2. TIME ETC.

Time Etc. is a virtual assistant agency consisting of only American natives. After a brief interview, this service matches you with a remote assistant to meet your business needs, at a reasonable monthly cost. In order to ease you into the process, Time Etc. provides a free one-hour trial. 10 hours per month will likely be enough for most tasks, since all these assistants are extremely talented. Each assistant in the roster works full-time as an assistant for multiple clients simultaneously and is available during designated times for phone calls and emails. Of all the available virtual assistant services that I have experienced, Time Etc. is the most professional and has impressed me the most – they've transformed the awkward "stranger hiring" process into a pleasant experience.

3. HIRE SOMEONE YOU KNOW

The third method for hiring an assistant is to hire someone you trust within your network. This is the most expensive option, but also yields the greatest results for complex tasks. I've personally found this method to yield the most valuable results because my assistants have had a blend of experience in music production and marketing communication skills. This combination has freed me to hire assistants to complete communication tasks through the lens of a composer or to create music projects through the perspective of a marketer. These tasks cost more than the other options, but I prefer the simplicity and higher return on investment.

ACTION STEPS

1	Have I systemized and automated as many business tasks as possible?
2	How valuable would an assistant be for my business growth?
3	What is one regular task I have that can be hired out to an assistant soon?

SECTION SUMMARY

If you've read *PART 5: Music Business Growth* and followed the Action Steps, then you've successfully established healthy work and growth habits, prepared yourself to prevent Creative Burnout, started practicing vital networking skills, and determined the value of internships and assistants in your career.

You're now ready to implement more advanced strategies into your business for faster growth. Move on to *PART 6: Music Business Strategies.*

PART 6

MUSIC BUSINESS STRATEGIES

22

WRITING A MUSIC CONTRACT?

The moment has finally come – a client wants to hire you to compose music for their project. During the excitement, it's important to stay level-headed and negotiate through the lens of a business owner. You need to earn a profit from this job and you need to stay on schedule while managing other projects.

Here enters the music contract – a small written agreement that outlines all expectations of the project between the creator and composer. This contract assures that both you and the creative team agree to fair and mutually beneficial terms. Here is the template I use on almost every new project:

AGREEMENT BETWEEN **STEVEN MELIN** ("COMPOSER") AND **JARVIS WADE** ("DEVELOPER") RE: MUSIC TRACKS FOR THE VIDEO GAME **"TALES OF INFINITY"**

1. SERVICES: Steven Melin ("Composer") shall compose, record, produce, mix, and deliver ***4 tracks***, totaling a ***minimum of 6 minutes and a maximum of 7 minutes in length***, of Original Music ("Tracks") for the VIDEO GAME **"TALES OF INFINITY"** ("Game") subject to the creative decisions of the Composer and **Jarvis Wade** ("Developer") during the process. Specific track list consists of:

1. *Main Theme*
2. *Ice Cave Theme*
3. *Battle Theme*
4. *Victory Theme*

2. DELIVERY REQUIREMENTS AND DATES:

a. Composer shall provide first-draft of *Main Theme* track for consideration to the Developer by ***February 19, 20xx;***

b. Developer shall provide feedback on *Main Theme* track to the Composer by ***February 26, 20xx***;

c. Composer shall make changes (if necessary) and deliver the final audio mix of *Main Theme* track in the agreed-upon format by ***March 15, 20xx;***

d. Composer shall provide remaining first-draft tracks (*Ice Cave Theme, Battle Theme, Victory Theme*) for consideration to the Developer by ***April 22, 20xx;***

e. Developer shall provide feedback on remaining tracks (*Ice Cave Theme, Battle Theme, Victory Theme)* to the Composer by ***May 2, 20xx***;

f. Composer shall make changes (if necessary) and deliver the final audio mixes ("Tracks") in the agreed-upon format by ***May 31, 20xx.***

3. COMPENSATION/PACKAGE FEE: The Compensation shall be a three-payment package fee totaling **USD$XXXX** and includes all costs for writing, recording, producing, mixing, and delivering the Tracks. Payment schedule:

1) **USD$XXX** to be delivered by ***February 15, 20xx*** as an upfront fee for *Main Theme* track;

2) **USD$XXX** to be delivered by ***March 15, 20xx*** after the receipt of *Main Theme* track; payment includes upfront fee for remaining tracks (*Ice Cave Theme, Battle Theme, Victory Theme*);

3) **USD$XXX** to be delivered by ***June 15, 20xx*** after the receipt of all remaining Tracks (*Ice Cave Theme, Battle Theme, Victory Theme*).

Composer shall email an invoice to Developer for each required payment. If PayPal is agreed as the chosen service for Compensation, an additional 3% charge will be added to each payment amount (totaling **USD$XXX**, **USD$XXX**, and **USD$XXX** respectively for each of the three payments).

4. SCREEN CREDIT: Composer shall receive single-card screen credit of the same duration, font and size as the Developer and shall share the same format (i.e., End Credits) as that of the Developer. Composer screen credit shall read as follows: **Music by Steven Melin**.

5. OWNERSHIP OF TRACKS: Composer shall own all rights to the Tracks and therefore shall be entitled to collect 100% of the writer and 100% of the publisher shares of public performance royalties (as that term is commonly used in the music industry) directly from the relevant performance rights organization(s). Composer is entitled to distribute and sell Tracks, in exclusive association with the Game, for profit in online music stores (i.e., iTunes, Spotify, Amazon, BandCamp etc.).

6. <u>RIGHTS OF DEVELOPER</u>: Developer shall have the perpetual, irrevocable license to use the Tracks in connection with any and all exploitation of the Game and its associated Intellectual Property in all media, including advertising and promotion of the Game. All rights in this agreement are assignable by Developer to a distributor, however Developer shall remain primarily liable for any obligations under this agreement.

7. <u>WARRANTIES AND REPRESENTATIONS</u>: Composer hereby makes customary representations and warranties as to the originality of the Tracks, that the Tracks violate no rights of any third party, that there will be no liens or encumbrances on the Tracks, and that the Developer shall be free to use the Tracks in the Game and the exploitation thereof.

If the above is correct, please sign below. Once fully signed, this will constitute our agreement.

APPROVED AND ACCEPTED:

Composer: **Steven Melin**   Developer: **Jarvis Wade**

(signature)   (signature)

Date: **X/X/XX**   Date: **X/X/XX**

Note that in just a few short pages, I outline the service I will conduct, delivery requirements and dates, compensation, screen credit, track ownership, rights of the creative team, and legal representation. In some cases, clients will provide their own written agreement. In all cases, you should fully understand all terms before agreeing.

Contracts increase professionalism, outline clear expectations, and improve all business relationships. Entering into any verbal agreement without documentation to back up expectations adds unnecessary risk to your business. Without a contract, it's too easy for one party to forget specific details weeks or months into the project. This is particularly important for projects that drag on for years, such as video game soundtracks.

Contracts increase professionalism, outline clear expectations, and improve all business relationships.

Using a template can significantly speed up the agreement process and in many cases earn you more (if not all) of your proposal when you create it yourself and ask the receiving party to agree to your terms. Almost all my contracts are agreed to, signed, and exchanged by email within one to two business days, often only requiring one revision to acknowledge a slight counter offer or adjusted delivery dates. When possible, I suggest asking for payment upfront and I always allow my clients to pay a final amount upon receipt and approval of all deliverables. Some trusted repeat clients prefer the ease of making one lump sum upfront payment for a project, but you should expect a minimum of two total payments (upfront and after final approval) with new clients. Steer clear of any projects and clients that won't agree to at least half payment upfront before any services are started. Failure to do this is a red flag of troubles to come.

I'm not an attorney, so consider my advice as opinion. This template may help many of you, but you should always consult legal counsel for your specific situation.

Download this free Music Contract template at:
www.stevenmelin.com/musiccontract

CONCLUSION

Now that you've learned how to write an effective music contract, you're ready to learn how to send a music invoice…

ACTION STEPS

1	How effectively have music contracts served my previous projects (if applicable)?
2	How will I benefit most from using a music contract on my next project?
3	How can I better prepare for my next project with a personalized music contract template?

23

SENDING A MUSIC INVOICE?

Once you've agreed to a music contract, it's important to send timely invoices to receive payments. Invoices save you time, earn you more money, and keep clients on schedule. In many cases one upfront or backend payment will suffice, but for other projects you will need to send multiple invoices based on the compensation dates outlined in the written agreement.

My favorite free platform for invoice management is **PayPal**. Its simple interface allows you to create and store a database of all client invoices. You can generate tax forms and statements at any time and PayPal only earns a 3% commission on every payment. To ensure that invoicing never costs you, I suggest that you add a *3% PayPal Fee* line item in every invoice. Of all my projects, I've only had a couple clients request to pay by check or their preferred payment service to avoid the fee. In any case, *I don't have to pay it*, nor do you. Quick online payments are a convenience for your client, and you should expect them to pay for it or choose an alternate payment source that costs you nothing extra.

> Invoices save you time, earn you more money, and keep clients on schedule.

Use the free **PayPal Fee Calculator**:
www.thefeecalculator.com

CONCLUSION

Now that you've learned how to send a music invoice, you can skip to *Chapter 25: Training for Professional Composing Speed*. If you're a film composer, read on to learn how to prepare for a film Spotting Session...

ACTION STEPS

1	How effectively have invoices served my previous projects (if applicable)?
2	How will I benefit most from using an invoice on my next project?
3	How can I better prepare for my next project with a personalized invoice template?

24

PREPARING FOR A FILM SPOTTING SESSION?

Spotting Sessions are one of the most important responsibilities for a film composer. Preparing incorrectly can cost you social credibility and future gigs, but nailing it can be a serious boost to your career and perception with clients.

A Spotting Session is a closed viewing of a film that occurs after *Production* and initiates *Post-Production*, the final editing phase of filmmaking once a film has been locked. This locked *Final Cut* of a film means that there will be no more changes to any scene lengths (unless critically necessary) – this is crucial for a composer, who needs to base all music decisions off this stationary version of the film. Topics of discussion during a Spotting Session include musical direction, specific genres, instrumentation, and the parts of the film that should and should *not* include music. This crucial meeting is a powerful moment for connecting to the filmmakers' vision for the film.

Spotting Sessions consist of the creative inner circle of the film production team (usually no more than five people), including the director, producers, and the film editor. Don't wait and risk losing credibility with your client. Set yourself up for success and prepare with these three steps:

1. WATCH THE FILM BEFORE THE SESSION

This seems like a no-brainer, but it's amazing how few composers do this. The spotting session is not the time to see the film for the first time. That screams *unprofessional*, especially if the director has sent you the movie with the sole purpose of you viewing it.

In my experience, it's best to watch the film at least twice. The first time is all about internalizing. Soak in the plot, cinematography, characters, dialogue, emotions, story… everything. Let it churn and marinate in your subconscious mind. For the second viewing, make sure you have pen and paper in hand. It's time to get down to business…

2. TAKE NOTES

When you're watching the film for the second time, jot down notes about *anything* and *everything* that comes to mind from a musical perspective. A few examples of helpful items to record:

- Instrumental ideas: warm strings here, soft flute there
- Motifs: uplifting theme for Sally, tragic theme for Francis
- Timecodes: brass comes in during chase scene at 1:23:02
- Types of music: string trio, full orchestra, solo piano

Once complete, analyze your notes and notice any recurring or familiar themes. The purpose of this step is to enter the Spotting Session with ideas of your own and to prepare for composing demos.

3. COMPOSE DEMOS

I can't recommend this enough. There is no better way to impress a director or producer than by entering the Spotting Session with actual musical demos in hand. Think about it – when the director wants to work with a composer on her next project, whose name will pop into her head first? The composer who was professional, timely, and *prepared.*

As a bonus, since the editor will be present with the film session open and ready to go, they can drop your music into the timeline and see how it feels against the film itself. This is incredibly helpful for receiving detailed feedback early.

There's nothing worse than thinking that the director wants one thing, pouring hours into your music, and then realizing that it doesn't fit their vision at all. Imagine sailing a large ship on the ocean that veers off course by two degrees. Initially, the small error is undetectable, but by the end of the journey your stop will be miles away from your destination. That's the result of a lack of alignment between the composer and filmmaker, and it's one of the many helpful ways that preparing demos in advance can save you a substantial amount of time in the long run.

DON'T SPEAK UNLESS SPOKEN TO

Usually, people speak mindlessly when nervous. If you're professional, prepared, and confident, you don't need to speak. Your copious notes and demo will speak for you. Obviously, if somebody asks for your opinion, gladly give it. The important thing to remember is that silence is a signal that you're confident in your handiwork. It may earn you serious respect with the filmmakers. If you disagree at a certain point, don't bring it up during the Spotting Session and interrupt the flow of the film. Instead, jot it down and gently mention the issue to the creators afterward. They are the final decision makers. If they veto your suggestion, remember that *you're being paid to serve their vision*, not the other way around.

Serving the film is your top priority. This film is not a showcase for your newest sample library or another feather in your cap for your demo reel – it's a piece of art that likely has a lot of blood, sweat, and tears poured into it. Your job is not to overshadow the film, but to *underscore* it. Sometimes that even means no music at all.

Your job is not to overshadow the film, but to underscore it.

CONCLUSION

Now that you've learned how to prepare for a film Spotting Session, you're ready to learn how to train for professional composing speed...

ACTION STEPS

1	How effectively did my music serve the vision of my last film (if applicable)?
2	Have I participated in a Spotting Session before? If so, was that a positive experience for everyone?
3	How can I better prepare for my next Spotting Session?

25

TRAINING FOR PROFESSIONAL COMPOSING SPEED?

Composing at a professional speed is critical for scaling your business. Speed is crucial for delivering music on time, increasing your project capacity, and charging fair rates. I currently compose at a speed of one minute of finished music for every three hours of work. This speed is consistent and reliable. On any given work day, I can reliably produce two minutes of music. I'm capable of producing three to five minutes if needed but doing so will affect the balance of my family schedule and other projects. This is extremely useful information, because it allows me to charge an accurate rate for my time and output capacity when I'm asked to score a project.

If I receive a last-minute call for a custom score due in two days and my schedule is already full of projects, my two options are to turn down the project or to fit it into my schedule and charge a premium for flexibility. I've done both and either decision can build rapport with your clients. Do what's right for you in each case.

Speed is crucial for delivering music on time, increasing your project capacity, and charging fair rates.

Here are four strategies for increasing your composition speed:

1. BE DECISIVE

Composers struggle with developing and finishing tracks due to indecision. With modern technology, there are countless decisions to make: what DAW to use, what samples to choose, what instruments to write for, what composition style to write in, notation versus recording...and all this *before* composing a note. The best way to be productive with your time is to make decisions...period! Art is subjective and we all grow through experience, so there really is no *right* or *wrong* process – there are effective and ineffective processes. Making quick decisions leads to faster writing. If your client doesn't like your first attempt, try again. You'll improve in time. When in doubt, ask a mentor or other composer friends to listen to your work for feedback and adjust from there.

Setting up DAW templates in advance can save you a considerable amount of time when starting new projects. At the time of this writing, I only have two templates that I use for every project – 1) a chiptune video game template, loaded with my favorite go-to video game synths and samplers, and 2) a massive orchestral film template, loaded with every articulation of strings, brass, woodwinds, percussion, vocals, ethnic woodwinds, ethnic strings, and synths. Whenever I load my film score template, there is already a piano track enabled in order to compose immediately. This limitation eliminates the need to choose an instrument. After writing a line, I can move the MIDI region directly to another instrument or I can pick another instrument to compose with, so long as I *make a decision.*

2. USE REFERENCE TRACKS

Whenever you start a project, you should ask the client to supply two to three reference tracks, sometimes called *temporary (temp) tracks*. These tracks reflect the sound your client is seeking, so it's helpful to add these tracks to your DAW session and extract as much information as possible – meter, tempo, key, instrumentation, location of section changes, etc. These notes will significantly speed up your workflow by providing you with practical musical structure. Theoretically, so long as you stay within the average parameters of the reference tracks provided, you can compose just about any notes and still please the client. This is especially true when delivering large amounts of music for projects such as a feature film or multiple episodes in a show series.

3. PREPARE LIVE INSTRUMENTS

Another way to become much faster at composing is to prepare live instruments for recording. If possible, try to equip your studio with quick access to all your live instruments. Ideally, all instruments should be within arms-reach, unpacked, and ready to record immediately. If not, ideas may come to you, but you will likely forget them during the five to ten minutes of unpacking and preparing your instrument. While sitting at my workstation, I can reach keyboards, guitars, electric bass, harps, violin, mandolin, woodwinds, and an auxiliary percussion box filled with sticks, metals, woods, shakers, ethnic instruments, and other knick-knacks collected over the years. All these instruments are instantly accessible and live beside my trusty microphone, ready to record at any moment. This level of accessibility promotes quick composing. I can record a live shaker with greater quality and musicality faster than I can find a shaker sample that I like. I can record a guitar lick or violin melody quicker than massaging mod wheel and velocity automations in my DAW. Live instruments matter and can greatly enhance the speed, efficiency, and creativity of your studio workflow.

4. PRACTICE

The fourth way to improve your composition speed is to practice composing daily with a timer. For optimum results, I suggest composing three hours a day with a countdown timer; stop when the timer ends and log your progress. This could be as simple as a sticky note or complex as a **Microsoft Excel** spreadsheet, but the purpose is to establish a habit of logging progress to achieve a faster average composing speed. I encourage you to aim for the average speed goal of one minute of music produced for every three hours. This is a very attainable goal for every composer and can be achieved with diligent daily practice. I suggest three hours a day because three hours is generally considered to be a session of Deep Work. In three hours, you can compose a meaningful amount of music that will move your business needle forward.

This daily practice needs to be undistracted, uninterrupted time. For many of you, an early morning or late-night session will work best because you have a 9–5 job or kids to take care of. For others, you may need to dedicate practice to the weekend. In any case, a higher frequency and consistency of practice sessions will have a direct impact on the improvement of your composing speed.

ACTION STEPS

1	How fast do I currently write music? Is this speed consistent and reliable?
2	What barriers are keeping me from composing faster?
3	What is one action I can take today to increase my composing speed?

SECTION SUMMARY

If you've read the entire book up to this point and have followed the Action Steps, then you've successfully found your Why, laid the foundation of a successful music composition career, created multiple means of recurring monthly income, equipped your music studio with the most effective hardware and software, established habits for business growth, and have implemented business strategies for scaling faster. You are now well on your way to a long-term successful career.

Move on to *PART 7: Next Steps* for practical next steps to take, including building a demo reel and portfolio, interacting with community, deeper training opportunities, private coaching, sponsorships, and how to establish your authority on social media.

PART 7

NEXT STEPS

BUILDING A DEMO REEL AND PORTFOLIO

The first step to building a career is sharing your brand with the world. As discussed earlier, a demo reel is a vital piece for captivating your audience when they visit your website. Crafting unique demo reels for specific job opportunities can help convince potential clients that you're the right composer for the project. Demo reels showcase the best of your music and should be crafted with your audience in mind. I suggest choosing three music tracks around two to three minutes in length that represent the types of projects you desire to work on in the future. Alternatively, you can use video clips from multiple projects in a five to seven-minute showreel (this is usually more impressive).

The easiest way to create a demo reel is to upload music tracks to a free **Soundcloud** account and embed the playlist directly on your website or share the URL in an email with a potential client. For video demo reels, I suggest editing in **Da Vinci Resolve** (free editing software) and uploading as one video to **YouTube**. You can embed this video directly on your website or share the URL in an email with a potential client.

A portfolio is your entire body of work. It's important to make this fully accessible to potential clients who want to dive deeper into your music. Platforms for showcasing your albums include your personal website, **Soundcloud**, **Bandcamp**, and **Soundrop**, among many others. My goal is to earn revenue on every asset I create, so I distribute all my music through Soundrop to reach as many ears as possible while earning additional income. I prefer to build my audience *while* earning passive income.

If you find yourself lacking custom scoring gigs, you can still create albums from previously composed tracks or create new albums to share. Always be working, even if you're not currently hired on an active project.

INTERACTING WITH COMMUNITY

A professional career as a music composer is often very isolating. It's important for you to find a supportive community of composers to challenge and encourage you along your journey. This is why I created the free private **Facebook** group Sonic Storytellers. In this group, we actively share resources to build our music businesses, critique each other's work, collaborate on projects, and encourage one another.

Join the free **Sonic Storytellers Group** today:
www.stevenmelin.com/sonicstorytellers

DEEPER TRAINING

The purpose of this book is to give you the essential training needed to build a successful screen music composition business. For you, this text may be the best possible resource for moving forward in your career. Others are visual learners, audio learners, or need hands-on-materials. However you prefer to learn, I encourage you to check out my other resources to learn this information in the way that serves you best:

Join me on **YouTube** for weekly Music Business videos:
www.stevenmelin.com/youtube

Listen to the **Sonic Storytellers Podcast**
for Music Business training: www.stevenmelin.com/podcast

Enroll in my Best-Selling **Udemy courses** for deeper music composition training, practical exercises, and additional resources:
www.stevenmelin.com/courses

PRIVATE COACHING

With 14 years of screen music industry experience, I've learned that there are four pillars that create a successful career: Music Composition, Music Production, Music Technology, and Music Business. In my time coaching thousands of composers, I've noticed that most composers tend to focus on only one or two of the four pillars, leaving a gaping hole in their craft.

What made the difference for me? *Mentorship* with industry pros. For thousands of years before us, blacksmiths, tailors, and engineers have passed their trades to apprentices. They understood what many have forgotten today – some skills and wisdom must be passed on privately. Since college, I'm grateful to have had not one, but *six* A-List composers pour into my career: **Garry Schyman** (*Middle-earth: Shadow of Mordor, Bioshock)*, **Penka Kouneva** (*The Mummy* VR, *Prince of Persia: The Forgotten Sands*), **Joel Goodman** (*American Experience, Being Elmo*), **Grant Kirkhope** (*Banjo Kazooie, GoldenEye 007*), **Jason Graves** (*Tomb Raider, Dead Space*), and **Austin Wintory** (*The Banner Saga, Journey*).

Your career is in your hands. How have you recently invested in your composition skills? Production mastery? Technical proficiency? Business growth? Through my **9-week Private Coaching program**, I'll take you to the next level of your career. We'll set goals together, create an action plan, and I'll hold you accountable.

> Learn more about **Private Coaching** at:
> www.stevenmelin.com/privatecoaching

SPONSORSHIPS

One of the best habits I've developed in my music business is forming personal relationships with sample instrument companies. When I compose demos on **YouTube Live** streams featuring new sample instruments, I exchange my time and influence for free products. Sample instrument companies are happy to provide digital goods in exchange for the exposure, because it lands them more sales at no cost to them. On top of free high-end products, these sponsorships also provide authority with my audience and attract new viewers, especially if my demos are used on the product sales pages. This is also a great revenue source through YouTube ads and if the company agrees to an affiliate marketing deal. As I build stronger relationships with each company, they are more willing to contact me about upcoming products and unique affiliate commissions.

At the time of this writing, 10% of my income consists of affiliate market revenue from multiple sample instrument companies. YouTube Live videos from several years ago continue earning me income every month as new viewers purchase products that I recommend. Free products, more influence, more income…all in exchange for a small amount of time and energy. Sponsorships have been an incredible addition to my business growth.

How do you get sponsorships? I don't recommend actively seeking them out; instead, I suggest you build your authority on social media to attract sponsors to you. When you seek out sponsorships, you appear desperate – the best-case scenario will be one product sponsorship, but you'll likely forfeit building an organic business relationship. When sponsors notice you as an authority in their industry, they'll reach out because they know that you provide value to them and their audience. This is *exactly* where you want to be. These sponsorships often turn into multiple future deals and help pave a consistent source of revenue in your business.

ESTABLISHING AUTHORITY ON SOCIAL MEDIA

Social media presence is a powerful tool for scaling your business. Social platforms provide direct access to interact with your clientele and influence them to make purchasing decisions…all for free! However, no one is going to buy your products or services without first trusting you and your brand. Without social proof and established credibility, you will have a hard time earning income from your marketing efforts.

Here are three ways to establish your authority on social media:

1. CONSISTENCY

Above all, consistency on social media platforms has the highest impact on your social influence. Most composers feel like they must spend hours producing high-quality content before posting on social media. While high-quality content is certainly useful for long-form platforms such as **YouTube,** daily micro-content on short-form platforms has a higher return on investment. The goal of social media is to capture attention of your client base. By posting a picture and caption or link each day, you remain in the forefront of your clients' minds. When you have constant, daily activity on social media, your clients feel close to you and are considerably more willing to contact you. Since it usually takes about 10 touch points before a potential client contacts you for business, you might as well speed up that process to only a week or two if you're posting every day.

2. RELEVANCE

It's crucial to be active every day on social media platforms, but *what* you post has equal value. As with any business, it's important to determine who your target audience is and to customize all content towards their problems and needs. It's also imperative to speak the language of each platform – to post *native* content on each:

Facebook is a question-and-answer text platform, so it's an amazing place to ask questions and interact with your audience directly. I suggest asking questions that reveal the specific needs of your audience. Use this information to generate your next product or service. **Facebook Live** is also a useful feature for live Q&A with your audience. On the contrary, Facebook is a terrible platform for posting links or videos. Facebook's feed algorithm punishes links that send users away from Facebook and highly compresses all audio and video. Use Facebook for what it excels at.

Instagram is a picture or short-form video platform. Instagram Stories are an incredible way to share the day-to-day aspects of your life without having to spend any extra time or energy. Stories are designed to be raw and unedited, so use this to your advantage. Users watch Instagram Stories to get a snapshot of your day, so this is by far the easiest platform to incorporate into your branding. Be sure to include relevant hashtags in all your picture or video posts. This is how people will discover your profile and follow you.

Twitter is a link-sharing platform. Due to its 280-character limit per post, brevity is king. Twitter is the best platform for sharing your resources – new blog posts, new YouTube videos, new products and services, etc. Whenever you post, get straight to the point and share a link. Like Instagram, be sure to include relevant hashtags in all your posts. For bonus views, tag other people in most, if not all, of your posts.

YouTube is a long-form video platform. While other platforms excel at 10-60 second videos due to quick consumption speed of users, YouTube rewards channels who retain viewership for long periods of time. When creating videos, aim for 7–16-minute length, averaging around 10 minutes per video. If you choose to create longer videos, take advantage of YouTube Live streams, which rank considerably higher than non-live videos in search. If you choose to upload videos to YouTube, I suggest a frequency of no less than one video per week. YouTube videos require time and effort, so it's highly impractical to post multiple videos per week when starting out. Consistency is still paramount, so one video per week is plenty.

3. INTERACTION

Consistency and relevance will generate a social influence, but without deliberate interaction, your social presence will lack personal connection. This third element has a profound impact on your success. Be someone who responds to *every* comment and direct message. How can you do this? I suggest scheduling one hour every two or three days for responding to your audience. Sometimes you'll have five responses; other times you'll have 50. One hour is usually more than enough time to answer these in bulk. In most cases, you can respond with a simple "thank you". Many times, you'll have the opportunity to respond with a link to one of your products or services that solves a problem. I've sold hundreds of courses and library tracks from these direct responses on social media platforms. I make a point to never respond to any connection with more than a few sentences. If a question requires more time than that, I will request a phone call or Facebook video chat to find a custom solution (which almost always leads to paid work!). Sticking to these boundaries saves me time and solves the problems of my audience.

Note that I don't respond immediately to comments and messages. That's a *waste of time*. If I were to interrupt my work day 20 times to give one response, I would burn an hour or two each day...not to mention the collateral damage of lost focus on other projects during those times. Social media should never be a distraction. Set aside intentional time to invest in your influence and connect with your audience.

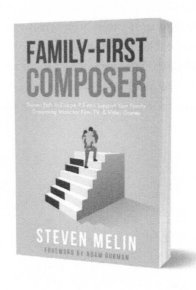

THANKS FOR READING!

I sincerely appreciate all your feedback and I love hearing from you.

I need your input to make the next version of this book and future books better. Please leave a helpful review on Amazon and share your thoughts of this book. Thank you!

– Steven Melin

Made in the USA
Monee, IL
18 August 2020